Discovering
Your Career Destiny

Career Plan for Your Life Revealed

Blueprints for Success

Dennis J. Caruso

Discovering Your Career Destiny

Career Plan for Your Life Revealed

Copyright © 2015 by Dennis J. Caruso

ISBN10: 1516942051
ISBN13: 9781516942053

DEDICATION

To my wife, *Lynn*, and my daughter, *Lauren*,
who supported and encouraged me in writing this book.

Contents

PREFACE..1

    Blueprints for the Perfect Career 1

FOREWORD 3

    How to Use This Book 3

CHAPTER 1—CAREER DESTINY 5

    Finding a Direction 5

    Blueprint #1-1 How Do I Start? 6

    Worksheet 1-A Work Interests...8

    Worksheet 1-B Leisure Interests..9

    Worksheet 1-B Leisure Interests..11

    Worksheet 1-C Work Values..12

    Worksheet 1-C Work Values..14

    Free Assessment Tests...15

    Satisfying Moments 16

    Worksheet 1-D Satisfying Moment #1...17

    Worksheet 1-E Satisfying Moment #2..19

    Sample 1-A List of Action Verbs..21

    Worksheet 1-F Patterns 23

    Sample 1-B Satisfying Moment..25

    Transferable Skills 27

    Worksheet 1-G Skills..28

    Worksheet 1-H Traits 30

    Worksheet 1-I Strengths and Stretches 32

    Blueprint #1-2 Direction 33

    Worksheet 1-J Putting It Together 34

    Worksheet 1-K Sorting It Out 35

Blueprint #1-3 Making a Decision—Option #1 36

Sample 1-C Decision Making Pros and Cons Decision: Quit Current Job 38

Worksheet 1-L Pros and Cons Put It into Practice 39

Blueprint #1-3 Making a Decision—Option #2 40

Blueprint #1-4 Personal Mission Statement 49

Worksheet 1-M Your Legacy 50

Sample 1-D Your Legacy 51

Worksheet 1-M Your Legacy 52

Sample 1-E Personal Mission Statement 53

Worksheet 1-N Personal Mission Statement 54

CHAPTER 2—THE RÉSUMÉ **57**

Creating the Self-Portrait 57

Blueprint #2-1 What Goes into Writing a Résumé 59

Writing an Effective Résumé 61

Sample 2-A Chronological Résumé 65

Sample 2-B Functional Résumé 67

Sample 2-C Hybrid Résumé 69

Sample 2-D Self-Management Skills 71

Sample 2-E Functional Skills 73

Blueprint #2-2 Putting It All Together 74

Cover Letter— An Introduction to Your Résumé 77

Sample 2-F Cover Letter—Responding to an Ad 79

Sample 2-G Cover Letter—Unsolicited 80

Sample 2-H Just for Fun! 81

CHAPTER 3—MAKING CONTACTS **85**

Getting the Interview 85

Blueprint #3-1 Getting the Interview 86

Sample 3-A Networking Script 89

Sample 3-B Contact Worksheet 91

Sample 3-C Personal/Professional Contacts 92

Use of Social Media in Career Search 93

A Few Important Guidelines 94

List of Social Media for Career Search 95

Blueprint #3-2 Preparing for the Interview 110

Sample 3-D Questions to Ask 113

Sample 3-E Questions Interviewers Ask 114

Blueprint #3-3 The Interview 119

Blueprint #3-4 The Follow-Up 123

Sample 3-F Follow-Up Letter 125

CHAPTER 4—NEGOTIATION **127**

Successfully Reaching Agreement 127

Blueprint #4-1 Preparing for Negotiations 129

Worksheet 4-A Imagery for Negotiations 131

Worksheet 4-B Knowing and Believing in Yourself..132

Worksheet 4-C Establishing Your Needs 134

Blueprint #4-2 The Negotiation Process..135

Worksheet 4-D Questions You Might Be Asked 138

Sample 4-A Helpful Tips during Negotiations 139

Sample 4-B Negotiation Script during Interview 141

Blueprint #4-3 After the Negotiation 143

Sample 4-C Resignation Letter 145

Worksheet 4-E Negotiations Assessment 146

ABOUT THE AUTHOR **147**

PREFACE

Blueprints for the Perfect Career

When a builder follows a set of blueprints to construct a house, he must first start with a solid foundation. If not, nothing that he builds will stand! Throughout this book, we will explore different blueprints to assist you in finding the job/career that will make you prosperous and successful.

The most important skill you can acquire is to discover how to bring security to everything in life. Even more important than finding a job, is allowing the principles in this book to guide you through strategic career moves. The design of this book will help you do just that.

This book contains powerful tips with examples, scripts of what to say, and worksheets on:

> 1. How to inventory your skills and abilities.
>
> 2. How to write well-constructed résumés.
>
> 3. How to interview effectively.
>
> 4. How to negotiate the compensation you deserve.
>
> 5. How to discover the blueprint for your life.

Based on an average 40-hour workweek, 50 weeks per year, the average job spans 2,000 hours per year. Doesn't it make more sense to spend those 2,000 hours in meaningful, fulfilling employment than to spend them imprisoned in a job you hate? "Work" does not have to equal "pain." Great jobs and careers do exist.

If this is welcome news to you, then read on. You are in for an exciting journey!

FOREWORD

How to Use This Book

This self-study book will guide you step-by-step, in a blueprint format, to discovering your career destiny. Sequentially written, the book has a definite beginning and ending. Do not skip any sections or gloss over the information. Start at the beginning and complete all the blueprints and activities in their order. Doing so will make you better prepared mentally, emotionally, and physically for your job search.

Each chapter has samples and worksheets with activities and resources. Be sure to complete these activities and check out the suggested resources. This valuable information will help you to achieve your career purpose.

Please email the author at careerdestiny32@gmail.com to receive a printable PDF version of the worksheets.

CHAPTER 1—CAREER DESTINY

Finding a Direction

In order to understand your strengths, you first have to take an inventory of the things that you do well, naturally, and enjoy doing. However, just knowing your skills and abilities does not necessarily allow you to move in the direction best suited for you. For example, you might be a whiz at analyzing data, and this is a highly marketable skill, but through research you discover the use of this skill will require you to work mostly indoors. Through the exercises in this chapter, you discover your interests would be to work outdoors!

But it is also important to continue seeking guidance from people close to you, such as family, friends, and teachers, and also from your conscience. Finding and discovering your direction will involve diligent soul searching. Your interests and values will determine whether certain skills should play a central role in your career design.

In this chapter, you will complete a set of blueprints dealing with your personal assessment. You will also complete various work and leisure inventories. These completed exercises will help reveal your gifts, personality traits, talents, and career interests. They will culminate in the writing of your Personal Mission Statement.

Blueprint #1-1
How Do I Start?

MATERIALS NEEDED

Paper and pen

Chair, desk, and light

Quiet place

Copy of résumé (if you have one.)

PREP TIME

Five (5) to eight (8) hours

DIRECTIONS

- Choose a time and location where you will not be disturbed.

- This is a time for you to reflect on your past experiences: your personal and professional relationships.

- Your résumé will assist you in recalling experiences in past jobs.

- Read and complete the following forms in developing and understanding your gifts, talents, skills, and traits: (*Worksheets 1-A, 1-B, 1-C, 1-D, 1-E, 1-F, 1-G, 1-H, 1-I,* and *Samples 1-A, 1-B*).

- Summarize these forms to determine and reveal patterns in your abilities, likes, dislikes, and strengths and weaknesses. Set this summary aside.

- You will use this information later in developing your résumé, determining your career path, and for interviewing purposes.

SUMMARY

This blueprint is an extremely important step in the process of your job/career search. Take your time to work through and do not rush through it. Without generating the necessary information for your gifts, talents, skills, and traits, you will not be able to arrive at a finished product.

> *If your actions inspire others to dream more, learn more,*
> *do more and become more, you are a leader.*

—John Quincy Adams

Worksheet 1-A
Work Interests

Place an "**o**" in front of each work interest that appeals to you or gives you enjoyment. Place an "**x**" in front of each work activity that you prefer to avoid. Please email the author at careerdestiny32@gmail.com to receive a printable PDF version of the worksheets.

____Artistic or creative expression of feelings or ideas.

____Scientific research, discovering, collecting, and analyzing information about the natural world, and applying research findings to problems in medicine, life sciences, or natural sciences.

____Outdoor work with plants or mechanical principles applied to practical situations through the use of machines or hand tools.

____Industrial activities that are repetitive, concrete, and organized, conducted in a factory setting.

____Business activities that are organized and clearly defined, requiring accuracy and close attention, primarily in an office setting.

____Selling ideas and/or products to others, using a variety of personal persuasion and promotional techniques.

____Accommodating and catering to the wishes and needs of others, usually on a one-to-one basis.

____Humanitarian interests in helping others with their mental, spiritual, social, physical, or vocational needs.

____Leading and influencing others by using high-level verbal or numerical abilities.

____Performing physical activities before an audience.

What would you attempt to do if you knew you would not fail?

—Robert Schuller

Worksheet 1-B
Leisure Interests

Some of your volunteer or leisure activities could easily transfer to the workplace. Place a "+" in front of each activity that you enjoy during your leisure time.

____Acting in a play or amateur variety show.

____Advising family members on their personal problems.

____Announcing or emceeing a program.

____Applying first aid in emergencies, as a volunteer.

____Building model airplanes, automobiles, or boats.

____Building or repairing electronic equipment.

____Campaigning for political candidates or issues.

____Canning and preserving food.

____Carving small, wooden objects.

____Coaching children or youth in sports activities.

____Collecting experiments involving plants.

____Conducting house-to-house or telephone surveys for an organization.

____Cooking gourmet meals.

____Creating hairstyles for friends.

____Designing greeting cards or writing original verses.

____Developing film.

____Doing impersonations.

____Doing public speaking or debating.

____Entertaining at parties or other events.

____Grooming or training animals.

____Helping conduct physical exercises for disabled people.

____Making ceramic objects.

____Modeling clothes for a fashion show.

____Mounting and framing pictures.

____Nursing sick pets.

____Painting or drawing pictures.

____Painting the interior or exterior of a house.

____Playing a musical instrument.

____Raising money for worthy causes.

____Refinishing or reupholstering furniture.

____Repairing or assembling bicycles.

____Repairing plumbing in the house.

____Repairing the family automobile.

____Sewing clothes for family and friends.

____Shopping for quantities of items for an organization.

____Singing at weddings or in the church choir.

____Speaking on radio or television.

____Taking photographs.

____Teaching in Sunday school.

____Tutoring pupils in school subjects.

____Weaving rugs or making quilts.

____Writing articles, stories, or plays.

____Writing songs for club socials or amateur plays.

Worksheet 1-B
Leisure Interests

In the space below, compile a list of the 10 leisure activities that appeal to you the most. Rank them in order of enjoyment.

1.

2.

3.

4.

5.

6.

7.

8.

9.

10.

List below the two activities that you most want to avoid.

1.

2.

Worksheet 1-C
Work Values

Most jobs are a combination of likes and dislikes. In the list below, place an "**o**" in front of the values that describe you the best. Place an "**x**" in front of the values that do not describe you at all.

____Achieve status and respect in the community.

____Attract public attention.

____Be employed only at certain times of the year.

____Change my duties frequently.

____Choose my own hours of work.

____Compete with others.

____Decide for myself what work to do and how to do it.

____Direct, manage, or supervise the activities of others.

____Do work that requires physical activity.

____Earn a large amount of money.

____Follow established procedures requiring little change.

____Follow my sense of adventure by taking risks.

____Have day-to-day contact with the general public.

____Help people with their problems.

____I prefer to work in a job that allows me to:

____Influence the opinions and decisions of others.

____Personally convince others to take certain actions.

____Search for and discover new facts and develop ways to apply them.

____Take frequent trips.

____Teach or care for children.

____Think and reason a lot.

____Use authority to control and direct others.

____Use machines or equipment.

____Use my analytical ability with mathematics or statistics.

____Use my hands or hand tools.

____Use my imagination to find new ways to do or say something.

____Work outdoors.

Worksheet 1-C
Work Values

In the space below, list your five most important work values. Put the work value that is most important to you in the first space, the next most important in the second space and so on.

1.

2.

3.

4.

5.

List below the three values that you dislike the most.

1.

2.

3.

Free Assessment Tests

Provided below are websites for your convenience. These sites provide testing free of charge. When you take the tests, be certain to answer the questions honestly to reflect your gifts, personality, and career interests properly.

PERSONALITY

www.typefocus.com

www.testingroom.com

www.queendom.com

CAREER

www.careerkey.org

www.colorwize.com/CareerTestFirst.htm

www.careertest.net

SPIRITUAL GIFTS

http://www.spiritualgiftstest.com/test/adult

www.buildingchurch.net/g2s.htm

https://gifts.churchgrowth.org/cgi-cg/gifts.cgi?intro=1

Satisfying Moments

Introduction

On the next several pages, you will describe two of your most satisfying moments. Recall two occasions in which you solved a problem, achieved a goal, filled a special role, or completed a job that was especially satisfying, fulfilling, or enjoyable for you.

Ground Rules

- Make it fun!

- You may draw from every period and experience of your life.

- Select occasions that were significant to you, regardless of their significance to others.

- Select accomplishments that gave you pride, enjoyment, and satisfaction.

- Give concise, rich, step-by-step details of your accomplishments.

- Use action words (see *Sample 1-A*); state what you did, what problem you solved, what results you produced.

- Be brief; use no more than one page for each satisfying moment.

- Answer the questions following each narrative page. These answers will help you analyze your satisfying moments for those Knowledge, Skills, and Abilities (KSAs) that are most enjoyable for you.

- Plan to spend some time on this exercise.

Worksheet 1-D
Satisfying Moment #1

Write a descriptive paragraph of your satisfying moment.

Questions about satisfying moment #1

Why were you proud of this achievement?

Why did you enjoy this achievement?

What motivated you to achieve?

On this occasion what particular skills, talents, knowledge, or traits that employers desire did you exhibit?

What kinds of "things" (objects, equipment, machinery), if any, were involved in this satisfying moment?

What type of people (general public, doctors, children), if any, were involved in this satisfying moment?

What kind of work (research, analyze, compile), if any, did you do with this information?

Circle all the action verbs you used in describing your satisfying moment. These action verbs may be used when you develop your résumé. If you find yourself using the same verbs over and over, refer to the *List of Action Verbs* in this book.

Worksheet 1-E
Satisfying Moment #2

Write a descriptive paragraph of your satisfying moment.

Questions about satisfying moment #2

Why were you proud of this achievement?

Why did you enjoy about this achievement?

What motivated you to achieve?

On this occasion, what particular skills, talents, knowledge, or traits that employers desire did you exhibit?

What kinds of "things" (objects, equipment, machinery), if any, were involved in this satisfying moment?

What type of people (general public, doctors, children), if any, were involved in this satisfying moment?

What kind of work (research, analyze, compile), if any, did you do with this information?

Circle all the action verbs you used in describing your satisfying moment. These action verbs may be used when you develop your résumé. If you find yourself using the same verbs over and over, refer to the *List of Action Verbs* in this book.

Homework

Try to think of three more satisfying moments. The more moments you can remember, the more you will learn about yourself and the best design for your life. Complete these on a separate sheet of paper and refer to the questions.

After you have completed each of your satisfying moments, you will need to examine the patterns of your Knowledge, Skills, and Abilities (KSAs).

Sample 1-A
List of Action Verbs

Clerk	Helper	Leader	Researcher
Approved	Assessed	Achieved	Clarified
Arranged	Assisted	Coached	Collected
Catalogued	Clarified	Coordinated	Critiqued
Classified	Coached	Directed	Diagnosed
Collected	Counseled	Expanded	Evaluated
Compiled	Demonstrated	Guided	Examined
Dispatched	Diagnosed	Improved	Extracted
Generated	Educated	Pioneered	Identified
Implemented	Expedited	Ratified	Inspected
Inspected	Facilitated	Resolved	Interpreted
Monitored	Familiarized	Restored	Interviewed
Operated	Formed	Spearheaded	Investigated
Prepared	Motivated	Transformed	Organized
Processed	Referred		Reviewed
Purchased	Rehabilitated	**Manager**	Summarized
Recorded	Represented	Achieved	Surveyed
Retrieved		Assigned	Systematized
Screened	**Innovator**	Chaired	
Specified	Conceptualized	Delegated	**Teacher**
Tabulated	Created	Coordinated	Adapted
Validated	Customized	Developed	Advised
	Designed	Consolidated	Clarified
Communicator	Developed	Directed	Communicated
Addressed	Established	Analyzed	Demystified
Arbitrated	Fashioned	Contracted	Developed
Arranged	Founded	Evaluated	Enabled
Authored	Illustrated	Improved	Encouraged
Collaborated	Initiated	Increased	Evaluated
Developed	Instituted	Managed	Explained
Directed	Integrated	Organized	Facilitated
Drafted	Introduced	Oversaw	Informed
Edited	Invented	Planned	Instructed

Clerk	Helper	Leader	Researcher
Enlisted	Originated	Prioritized	Persuaded
Formulated	Performed	Procured	Set goals
Influenced	Planned	Produced	Stimulated
Interpreted	Revitalized	Recommended	Trained

Communicator	Engineer	Manager	Thinker
Mediated	Assembled	Review	Administered
Moderated	Built	Strengthened	Allocated
Negotiated	Calculated	Scheduled	Analyzed
Persuaded	Computed	Supervised	Appraised
Promoted	Designed		Audited
Publicized	Devised		Balanced
Reconciled	Engineered		Budgeted
Recruited	Fabricated		Calculated
Spoke	Maintained		Computed
Translated	Operated		Developed
Wrote	Overhauled		Forecasted
	Programmed		Marketed
	Remodeled		Planned
	Repaired		Projected
	Solved		Researched
	Upgraded		

Worksheet 1-F
Patterns

Look at your answers to the questions covering each satisfying moment. In the space below, list the **K**nowledge, **S**kills, and **A**bilities (example: leading a team) that appeared most frequently, in order of their frequency of use.

1.

2.

3.

4.

5.

Using action verbs, describe any patterns you see emerging from the list of KSAs you used most frequently.

KSAs You Enjoy

Look at your answers to the questions covering each satisfying moment. In the space below, list the **K**nowledge, **S**kills, and **A**bilities that you enjoy using, in the order of how much you like using them.

1.

2.

3.

4.

5.

Compare the list of **KSAs** that you use frequently with the list of **KSAs** that you enjoy. Do you see any overlap?

These **KSAs** should motivate you to give your personal best. In the space below, summarize the results of your reflection on the most satisfying moments of your life.

Sample 1-B
Satisfying Moment

"The Budget" was a terrible ordeal we had to endure every year. It began with the sales forecast, which I **created**. Eight different departments contributed information. With each contribution, I had to **revise** the original sales forecast. The entire process took two months from creation to approval, with at least nine major revisions in between.

I **organized** and **led** a team of eight people, each representing a department, and **redesigned** the entire budgeting process. I **coordinated** the efforts of each department, **developed** timing schedules, and **charted** the workflow.

The result: We **reduced** the total time spent creating the budget by four weeks.

Questions about Satisfying Moment (using the example)

Why were you proud of this achievement?

> I took the initiative to **create** a change.

Why did you enjoy this achievement?

> **Worked** in a team environment.

What motivated you to achieve?

> **Challenged** to **solve** a problem.

What particular skills, talents, knowledge, or traits that employer's desire was exhibited during this occasion?

> Organizing, leading, managing, creating, designing.

What kinds of "things" (objects, equipment, machinery) if any, were involved in this satisfying moment?

> Computer with budgeting, scheduling, and word processing software.

What type of people (general public, doctors, children), if any, were involved in this satisfying moment?

Internal department managers.

What kind of work (research, analyze, compile) did you do with information, if any?

Collected, reviewed, evaluated, organized, overhauled, and repaired.

Underline all the action verbs used in describing this satisfying moment. These action verbs may be used when you develop your résumé. *Note the* **bolded** *action verbs in the example.*

Transferable Skills

INTRODUCTION

Now that you have a good idea of the kind of **KSAs** that you use frequently and bring you enjoyment, it is time to see how these skills can be transferred to the workplace. Most functional or transferable skills can be sorted into the two, main categories listed below. This exercise is designed to enrich your list of **KSAs** with skills and abilities that transfer directly into the workplace.

1. A **SKILL** is achieved through practice, making you an expert. For example, you might be skilled in using Microsoft Excel.

2. A **TRAIT** is a distinguished quality you have in your personality. For example, you might have a personality trait of working well under time constraints.

Review the following lists of transferable skills and traits.

Place a "1" in front of the skills or traits that *strongly* characterize you.

Place a "2" in front of the skills or traits that describe you to a *large extent.*

Place a "3" in front of the skills or traits that describe you to *some extent.*

Worksheet 1-G
Skills

___ Communicating

___ Trouble shooting

___ Problem solving

___ Implementing

___ Analyzing/assessing

___ Self-understanding

___ Planning

___ Understanding

___ Decision making

___ Selling goals

___ Innovating

___ Conceptualizing

___ Thinking logically

___ Generalizing

___ Evaluating

___ Managing time

___ Identifying problems

___ Creating

___ Synthesizing

___ Judging

___ Forecasting

___ Controlling

___ Tolerating ambiguity

___ Organizing

___ Motivating

___ Persuading

___ Leading

___ Encouraging

___ Selling

___ Improving

___ Performing

___ Designing

___ Reviewing

___ Consulting

___ Attaining

___ Teaching

___ Team building

___ Cultivating

___ Updating

___ Advising

___ Coaching

___ Interpreting

___ Supervising

___ Achieving

___ Estimating

___ Reporting

___ Negotiating

___ Managing

___ Administering

___ Thinking critically

___ Collecting data

___ Visioning

___ Taking responsibility

Worksheet 1-H
Traits

___ Diligent

___ Honest

___ Patient

___ Reliable

___ Innovative

___ Perceptive

___ Persistent

___ Assertive

___ Tactful

___ Sensitive

___ Loyal

___ Astute

___ Successful

___ Risk taker

___ Versatile

___ Easy going

___ Enthusiastic

___ Calm

___ Out-going

___ Flexible

___ Expressive

___ Competent

___ Adaptable

___ Factual

___ Democratic

___ Receptive

___ Determining

___ Diplomatic

___ Resourceful

___ Self-confident

___ Creative

___ Tenacious

___ Open

___ Discrete

___ Objective

___ Talented

___ Warm

___ Empathic

___ Orderly

___ Analytical

___ Tolerant

___ Candid

___ Frank

___ Adventuresome

___ Cooperative

___ Firm

___ Dynamic

___ Sincere

___ Self-starter

___ Initiator

___ Precise

___ Efficient

___ Charismatic

___ Effective

Worksheet 1-I
Strengths and Stretches

Rank the order of the 10 characteristics on each list from *Worksheets 1-G, 1-H* that best describes you. Use a "1" for the characteristic that is most like you, a "2" for the one that is next most like you, and so on.

Skills	Traits
1.	1.
2.	2.
3.	3.
4.	4.
5.	5.
6.	6.
7.	7.
8.	8.
9.	9.
10.	10.

Review the previous worksheets and indicate below those *skills* and *traits,* if any, that you wish to use more. This will allow you to stretch and grow.

Skills	Traits
1.	1.
2.	2.
3.	3.
4.	4.
5.	5.

At this point, you should have a relatively clear picture of your current strengths, as well as an idea of the kind of skills and strengths you wish to utilize as you face future challenges.

Blueprint #1-2
Direction

MATERIALS NEEDED

Paper and pen

Chair, desk, and light in a quiet place

Work Interests *Worksheet 1-A*

Leisure Interests *Worksheet 1-B*

Work Values *Worksheet 1-C*

PREP TIME

Two (2) to four (4) hours

DIRECTIONS

- First, complete the exercises on your Work Interests, Leisure Interests, and Work Values (*Worksheets 1-A, 1-B, and 1-C*).

- Next, based on all the completed forms, it's time for you to sort out the information.

- Finally, complete *Worksheets 1-G, 1-H*.

SUMMARY

The previous *Blueprint #1-1* and this *Blueprint #1-2* are part of the base materials used in completing the other blueprints to come. These blueprints, once completed, will give you a better understanding of your skills, talents, abilities, God-given gifts, interests, and traits. The information obtained from these blueprints will also be useful when you have a face-to-face interview, as you will know where you have been, where you are presently, and where you are going.

Worksheet 1-J
Putting It Together

Review the previous exercises and cluster your knowledge, skills, abilities, work interests, leisure interests, and work values into categories. For example, you might have a cluster that reads, "teach, train, perform, show, demonstrate" or "create, design, adapt, modify."

List your clusters below.

1.

2.

3.

4.

5.

What patterns have emerged from these exercises?

Worksheet 1-K
Sorting It Out

You have done a tremendous amount of work so far. You have searched your past and analyzed it thoroughly. You have been asked to take note of the things you enjoy and some you do not enjoy. You might have discovered from the lists some things that intrigue you, or that you would like to be involved with in the future.

Sort these items into the following three categories.

1. Things I would like to keep doing.

2. Things I would like to start doing.

3. Things I would like to stop doing.

Read over what you have written.
Complete anything unfinished.

Blueprint #1-3
Making a Decision—Option #1

This section of blueprints has two options. As a praying man, I believe in the power of prayer and that God has a plan for our lives. If option #2 has not worked out for you or you're still searching for what your purpose is, then I strongly suggest trying option #1. Whatever your personal beliefs are, you can incorporate them in this blueprint.

MATERIALS NEEDED

Paper and pen

Binder to keep materials and notes organized

Chair, desk, and light

Quiet place

Friends, family, teachers, pastors, and others

PREP TIME

Three (3) to four (4) hours or until your direction is clear

DIRECTIONS

- **Compile**—On a piece of paper compile a list of the "pros" on the left side and the "cons" on the right side, as they relate to the decision you are considering (*Worksheet 1-L, Sample 1-C*).

- **Conviction**—Based on your "belief system," write your intuitive decision.

- **Communicating**—Write down what you believe God is communicating to you through prayer about the decision.

- **Counsel**—Seek godly counsel from a known religious or spiritual person. Do not seek advice from a person who is "good and moral," but from a godly individual. This individual would be someone you know who follows your spiritual teachings and walks in its same principles. This counsel should avoid someone's personal opinion.

- **Confirmation**—As you read your sacred scripture, watch for confirmation of the decision you need to make. God will speak to you. Be patient!

SUMMARY

Seeking God is and always should be the first step in your decision-making process. If we ask in faith, a plan will be revealed to us. The job/career for you will be revealed through this decision-making process.

Spend as much time as necessary in seeking a career plan for you. This is more important than putting your résumé together or trying to get interviews.

"For I know the plans I have for you," declares the Lord,
"plans to prosper you and not to harm you, plans to give you hope and a future."

—Jeremiah 29:11

Sample 1-C
Decision Making Pros and Cons
Decision: Quit Current Job

PROS	CONS
1. Reduce stress	1. Lack income
2. Will have time to find new job	2. Doesn't look good w/o a steady job
3. Will not have to compromise my beliefs	3. Might have to relocate
4. Don't like or enjoy current job	4. Lack job security
5. Could earn more	5. Insecurity for spouse/ family w/o regular income
6. Could pursue a career in construction management	
7. Could be first step in starting my own business	
8. Be challenged in something I love to do: *construction*	

Worksheet 1-L
Pros and Cons
Put It into Practice

Using a piece of paper, make a line down the middle. On the left, list "Pros" and on the right, list "Cons." At the top of the page write the decision you are considering.

PROS	CONS

Blueprint #1-3
Making a Decision—Option #2

MATERIALS NEEDED

Paper and pen

Binder to keep materials and notes organized

Chair, desk, and light

Quiet place

Friends, family, teachers, coaches, or any counselor you deem fit

PREP TIME

Three (3) to four (4) hours or until your direction is clear

Reboot Your Mind

After every few months, we reset our cell phones to update and optimize their overall performance. Or we reboot our computers to clear the cache memory.

The same is true with humans. For better decision making, we need to clear our minds of all worries, plans, sadness, and even happiness.

Before we begin this exercise of decision making, reboot your mind for 15 minutes by going into a literally "BLANK" state of mind.

DIRECTIONS

1. Identify the Decision under Evaluation

Once you are done with the soul searching, personality tests, and career analysis, you have arrived at a point of making a decision. This could be anything related to your career, for instance;

Quit current job and find a new one in the oil exploration industry,

OR

As a graduate just out of college, you have chosen to pursue your career in digital marketing, OR

You have decided to quit your current job and pursue an entrepreneurial career in technology, OR

You have decided to pursue a career in teaching "statistical inference" at the university level OR

any other decision.

Shortlist and jot down the single decision to be made.

2. Formulate Criteria for Evaluation

You must have arrived at this "single decision" after a series of analysis and research work. Gather all the clusters you had made before, summarize all the research findings, and formulate the criteria for advanced decision making.

Be straightforward and clear in defining your priority list. These are cautious moments of the final stages of your decision-making module. Clarity of priorities/criteria here is the ultimate key toward success.

We all should have a fairly good idea of what motivates us; listing them priority-wise will always reveal some new insights, as the visual will assist in the decision-making process.

List all the variables you deem relevant. Assign them a number out of 100 percent per their importance. Please note that the sum of all the variables must equal 100 percent.

For instance,

Variable Type	Percentage
Passion/Interest	20
Money	15
Distance from Residence	15
Job Security	10
Job Stress	10
Flexible Timings	5
Freedom of Belief and Practice	5
Discrimination-Free Employer	5
Designation—Label	5
Expected Growth	3
Authority	2
Perks	2
Benefits covering family	2
Indoor	1
Grand Total	**100 percent**

Once your priorities are set, then move on to the next step.

Words of caution: Variables/criteria will differ from person to person because we all have different priorities, likes, and dislikes. Your priorities will be ranked by the percentage assigned to the decisions-related variable; the higher the number, the higher the priority.

3. Identify Alternative Course of Actions

You have identified the decision you are evaluating. However, there should be a plan B, plan C, or the "**opportunity cost plan,**" that is, the second (apparently) best available course of action. Search online for more details about "opportunity cost."

Experts of decision making have always placed special emphasis on the idea that if Plan A is chosen, then, in both letter and spirit, Plan A must be better than the rest of the available choices. There should not be any gray areas. The feasibility of Plan A should easily outdo Plan B and other alternatives.

We can only reach this perfect state after comparing all the available courses of actions/options/alternatives with the criteria we have setup in step #2.

For instance, we have setup the following alternatives.

Plan	Type
Decision 1	Marketing Executive at P&G GLOBAL
Decision 2	Finance Analyst at Walmart
Decision 3	Entrepreneur in Technology
Decision x	Description X

4. Evaluate All Alternatives along with the Criteria.

List your "Criteria" along with all the "Alternatives" in the following fashion.

Variable Type	Percentage	Decision 1 Marketing Executive P&G Global		Decision 2 Finance Analyst Walmart		Decision 3 Entrepreneur Technology		Decision x Title Company	
		Rating	Total Score	Rating	Total Score	Rating	Total Score	Rating	Total
Passion/Interest	20	Score							
Money	15								
Distance from Residence	15								
Job Security	10								
Job Stress	8								
Flexible Timings	5								
Freedom of Belief and Practice	5								
Discrimination – free Employer	5								
Designation – Label	5								
Expected Growth	3								
Authority	2								
Perks	2								
Benefits covering family	2								
Indoor	3								
Grand Total	100 percent								

Next fill in the score for each alternative against the assigned variables and calculate the score. Scores are assigned between 0 and 10 with 0 being the least attractive for a particular option in relation to that variable and 10 being most attractive.

Variable Type	Percentage	Decision 1 Marketing Executive P&G Global		Decision 2 Finance Analyst Walmart		Decision 3 Entrepreneur Technology		Decision x Title Company	
		Rating	Total Score	rating	Total Score	rating	Total Score	rating	Total Score
Passion/Interest	20	10	2						
Money	15								
Distance from Residence	15								
Job Security	10								
Job Stress	8								
Flexible Timings	5								
Freedom of Belief and Practice	5								
Discrimination – free Employer	5								
Designation – Label	5								
Expected Growth	3								
Authority	2								
Perks	2								
Benefits covering family	2								
Indoor	3								
Grand Total	100 percent								

Your score is calculated by multiplying the percentage with the attractiveness points. For instance for Decision 1, the "Passion/Interest" variable, your score would be = 20 percent x 10 = 2.

Similarly fill in the complete table by assigning ratings and computing scores for all the available alternatives. If any variable does not apply to any of the alternative plans, mark "NA" for not applicable.

Variable Type	Percentage	Decision 1 Marketing Executive P&G Global		Decision 2 Finance Analyst Walmart		Decision 3 Entrepreneur Technology		Decision x Title Company	
		Rating	Total Score	rating	Total Score	rating	Total Score	rating	Total Score
Passion/Interest	20%	10	2	7	1.4	10	2	3	0.6
Money	15%	8	1.2	5	0.75	3	0.45	5	0.75
Distance from Residence	15%	7	1.05	9	1.35	2	0.3		0
Job Security	10%	6	0.6	3	0.3	6	0.6	5	0.5
Job Stress	8%	4	0.32	7	0.56	9	0.72	3	0.24
Flexible Timings	5%	7	0.35	3	0.15	2	0.1	2	0.1
Freedom of Belief and Practice	5%	6	0.3	2	0.1	1	0.05	5	0.25
Discrimination - free Employer	5%	9	0.45	9	0.45	5	0.25	2	0.1
Designation / Label	5%	4	0.2	3	0.15	2	0.1		0
Expected Growth	3%	8	0.24	1	0.03	2	0.06	2	0.06
Authority	2%	5	0.1	0	0	1	0.02	3	0.06
Perks	2%	2	0.04	3	0.06	1	0.02	2	0.04
Benefits covering family	2%	8	0.16	2	0.04	2	0.04		0
Indoor	3%	1	0.03	1	0.03	1	0.03	4	0.12
Grand Total	100 percent		7.04		5.37		4.74		2.82

Assign a rating and find the score of each variable against each alternative and sum up the total scores. The "Alternative" with the highest score is the most viable decision option for you.

Form a summary of the final scores.

Plan	Type	Final Score
Decision 1	Marketing Executive at P&G GLOBAL	7.04
Decision 2	Finance Analyst at Walmart	5.37
Decision 3	Entrepreneur in Technology	4.74
Decision x	Description X	2.82

Final scores imply that Decision #1 of a "Marketing Executive at P&G Global" would suit you the most because your advanced decision-making viability analysis supports the affinity between your priorities and the features of this particular decision.

Validation Check

It would be a good idea to review all the steps (step #1 through step #4) along with a counselor/expert/well-wisher and, with his/her help, try to redo these steps to be as unbiased and objective as possible. If the results are consistent with your findings, then well done! If not, then it would be highly suggested to prioritize the latter results against the former as latter analysis was done with another person for more accuracy.

Note: Always remember, at the end of the day, you will bear the consequences. So it is your decision. Follow your heart and own the decision! Final choices will always be yours!

However, if your primary motivator is Passion/Interest rather than Materialistic variables, in that case even if all your analyses are pointing you toward the "North Direction" and your Intuition is guiding you toward the "South Direction," then you should consider going with your gut feeling. As with all matters of the heart, you'll know when you find it. If you are getting this feeling for a particular direction, then go for it because right from the starting point, your personality type was inclined more toward essence and intuition than mere money and materialism. Therefore art, feelings, and emotions would better guide you than science. **Words of caution** are worth mentioning here: Almost all emotional and heart-making decisions do not work out in the long run. Remember you were designed with gifts and talents that will be rewarding and satisfying.

5. Implement Control and Review

Implement the final decision. If you are a job seeker, then keep applying for the top score alternative and divide your efforts accordingly. If you have planned to start your own business, then just do it. (Make sure you have an advanced monthly budget for at least five to six months.)

Keep up the hard work, as there is a great likelihood that you will land your desired career. However, the process for decision making does not end here. Very vigilantly, keep evaluating your selected alternative against the criterion variables that made you select this path. In this evaluation and review exercise, if deviation is standard, then there is nothing to worry about.

However, if the deviation variance is too wide and the criterion ranks high in your priority, then you might need to switch to Plan B or another alternative, because the very reason you chose Plan A is not applicable any more.

If you are seeking a new career opportunity, stay in your current job and **redo** the entire process.

SUMMARY

For quality decision making, analyze your internal strengths and weaknesses and compare them to available opportunities and threats. Try to capitalize on your strengths by matching them with the available opportunities in the external environment.

Once you have completed your personality analysis and identified your type, then shortlist the decision toward which you have a maximum inclination and follow the following steps;

- Identify the decision under evaluation

- Formulate the criteria for evaluation

- Identify alternative courses of action

- Evaluative alternatives

- Implement, control, and review

All this analysis will only guide you toward the apparent correct direction. However, these scientific analyses do not always apply. For instance, science cannot explain the purpose of our lives. Therefore, use this analysis as a guiding tool toward making the right direction for you.

At the end of the day, you will bear the consequences of your decision. So be mindful, follow your brain, and leave the final decision to your heart. If your heart and intuition are undecided, then follow the direction showed by the scientific analysis or go to Option #1 of Decision Making.

Blueprint #1-4
Personal Mission Statement

MATERIALS NEEDED

Paper and pen

Desk, chair, and light

Quiet place

All completed exercises from last blueprint

PREP TIME

Two (2) to three (3) hours

DIRECTIONS

- Develop a *Personal Mission Statement* that includes your vision of how you see yourself, what role/job you see for yourself, and how you plan to get there (*Worksheet 1-J, 1-K, Sample 1-E*).

- Don't shoot too high in setting your vision or role. Stretch, but be realistic.

- Based on the completed exercises and your personal mission statement, you should be ready to proceed to Chapter 2.

SUMMARY

In business, a mission statement is a short, descriptive statement of the common objective and focus of the organization. For the individual, a personal mission statement serves much the same purpose. It is a clear, concise statement defining how you plan to use your talents, skills, abilities, and gifts to contribute to an organization.

Worksheet 1-M
Your Legacy

Introduction

Before you take any kind of trip, you need to know where you are going and how you will get there. From the previously completed blueprints you will know which work-related interests, skills, abilities, and values describe you best as a potential employee. However, what about you as a person? Your personal values, vision, and mission have a direct impact on your future direction.

One of Stephen R. Covey's seven habits of highly effective people is to "Begin with the end in mind." Covey advises first describing yourself in the way you want most to be remembered, and then dedicating yourself to making that happen.

Answer these questions, as honestly as you can.

1. How would I most like to be remembered?

2. What do I need to do make this a reality?

Covey further suggests that you look at each of your "life roles" (husband, father, mother, sister, teacher, friend, employer, employee, neighbor, etc.). Our lives encompass so much more than work. We need to keep balance in our lives so that we are vital and productive in all aspects of living.

Sample 1-D
Your Legacy

Describe how you want to be *remembered* and how you want to *function* in each of your *life roles*. These are the things that are important to you.

Life Role #1: Husband

Description: Remembered as a dedicated and supportive husband. To provide my wife with the love, support, and encouragement needed for a long-term marriage.

Life Role #2: Father

Description: Remembered as a loving and supportive father. Raise my children in a godly way. Lead by example.

Life Role #3: Employer

Description: Remembered as an employer who helps people grow personally and professionally. Treat all employees fairly and equally. Compensate each employee justly.

Life Role #4: Neighbor

Description: Remembered as a neighbor who was friendly, helpful, and honest. Treat neighbors with respect and offer help if and when needed.

Life Role #5: Son

Description: Remembered as a son who always honored and respected his parents. Support elderly parents. Comfort and always show respect.

Worksheet 1-M
Your Legacy

Describe how you want to be *remembered* and how you want to *function* in each of your *life roles.* These are the things that are important to you.

Life Role #1

Description:

Life Role #2

Description:

Life Role #3

Description:

Life Role #4

Description:

Life Role #5

Description:

Sample 1-E
Personal Mission Statement

My mission is to seek guidance on how to use the gifts, talents, and knowledge I possess for the purpose of being a construction manager to increase the self-esteem and confidence of others, whether in a professional, personal, or volunteer capacity. I will act on opportunities with my values and standards in accordance with high integrity and purpose for my life.

Worksheet 1-N
Personal Mission Statement

As you described how you want to be remembered and how you want to function in each of your life roles, you were actually creating a statement of your personal values. Your values guide you in making decisions that affect your life.

Using this information, write your *Personal Mission Statement* in the space below. This is a personal statement: there is no one way to do this.

THE CROSSROADS

Several weeks after a young man had been hired, he was called into the personnel director's office. "What is the meaning of this?" the director asked. "When you applied for this job, you told us you had five years experience. Now we've discovered this is the first job you've ever held."

"Well," the young man replied, "in your advertisement you said you wanted somebody with imagination."

While your imagination can place you anywhere, reality will eventually take over. Do not let reality put you in a job you despise. The simplest way to avoid this is to seek guidance and counsel. The most important step in discovering your true career path is to allow those you trust and know to be part of your life's decision, including your next job.

If you are reading this book, most likely you have reached a crossroad in your life. Perhaps you are a fulltime mom facing an empty house as your children go off on their own, or you might be a college student facing graduation. You could be retiring from military service, or, as many are experiencing, you are being downsized out of a "secure" job that you have held for many years.

The reality is, since the war on terrorism began, our economy has been shaky and employment uncertain. This book will help you if you are unemployed, underemployed, or unhappily employed!

CHAPTER 2—THE RÉSUMÉ

Creating the Self-Portrait

Introduction

Do you remember school pictures? Have you ever had a professional photographer take a picture of you or your family? Remember how you styled your hair and wore your Sunday best? You wanted to look great in the photos because you would be sharing your pictures with others.

Well, the résumé is very much like a self-portrait. But the résumé reveals more than just a "snapshot" of you. It goes into greater detail; it is a real "close-up" of who you are. That's why it is so important to put your best into your résumé. It is literally your "foot" in the door, and if you "look" shabby on your résumé, potential employers won't even "let you in."

A résumé is more than just a list of past work experience; it is your sales pitch. However, some folks do not realize just how important the résumé can be. Take a look at some mistakes found on résumés.

Note: Please do not misconstrue my 14 jobs as "job-hopping." I have never quit a job.

Here are my qualifications for you to overlook. I procrastinate—especially when the task is unpleasant.

- Education: College, August 1890-May 1994.

- Instrumental in ruining the entire operation for a Midwest chain operation.

- It is best for employers that I not work with people.

- Personal interests: donating blood—fourteen gallons so far.

These silly mistakes show how important it is to check your spelling and to carefully read over your résumé. Take your time when you create your "self-portrait." Remember, you will be sharing it with others.

HOMEWORK

On a piece of paper, write three important items that should be included on your résumé. List them in order of importance. When you have completed this chapter, we will revisit your answers.

Successful and unsuccessful people do not vary greatly in their abilities.
They vary in their desires to reach their potential.

—John Maxwell

Blueprint #2-1
What Goes into Writing a Résumé

MATERIALS NEEDED

Paper and pen

Chair, desk, and light

Copy of résumé (if you have one)

Results from personal assessment worksheet (Chapter 1)

List of previous employers and jobs held

PREP TIME

Two (2) to four (4) hours

DIRECTIONS

- Decide on résumé format (*Samples 2-A, 2-B, 2-C*)—chronological, functional, or hybrid.

- For a Chronological Résumé, start with your most recent employment and work back.

- For a Functional Résumé, list your experiences and skill sets.

- For a Hybrid Résumé, combine areas of expertise with some employment history items.

- Separate your résumé into headers.

- Obtain all necessary information to include on your résumé for each header.

SUMMARY

Like recipes, what goes in could make all the difference. Leave an important ingredient out, and surely the end result will not be good. You could really spice it up and get the reviewer's attention, or downplay it and have a mild version. But, keep in mind that you want to get the attention of the person reading your résumé. Be sure to sprinkle in action verbs, along with specific functional and self-management skills.

The spice you need to add to make your résumé really stand out would be your successes and accomplishments. If you can "dollar-ize" your success, it will have a strong impact. For example: *Reduced operating expenses over previous year by more than $1.3 million.* Employers like to see dollar amounts you could save their company.

Money tends to drive the market place, but do not forget what should also drive you as you go through the employment process. Remember to pray and carefully consider what you do as you proceed through each step.

When putting your résumé together, take time to focus on your successes and accomplishments at each job you have had.

Writing an Effective Résumé

There are thousands of websites available that give you advice on how to write a résumé. This chapter will cover some basic guidelines to help you choose a résumé format and then look at ways to make your résumé stand out.

First, we'll look at what you want to put into your résumé. The content of your résumé is more important than substantial information about you, your successes, and accomplishments.

Second, we'll look at the three different résumé formats.

- Chronological

- Functional

- Hybrid (combination of Chronological and Functional)

Just as there are many different flavors of ice cream, there are just as many people, who for some reason do not like certain flavors. The same is true about résumés; different people like different formats, and they have strong opinions to back themselves up. If there is a certain flavor, or style format, that you wish to use to write your résumé, then use it.

To appeal to the taste of others, I would strongly suggest using two different styles. Remember, you are marketing your skills, talents, abilities, and experiences; so the more people you reach, the better your chances of getting an interview and job offer.

Chronological résumés are preferred over Functional most of the time, because they begin with your most recent work experience and proceed back. They also take less time to read and understand. (Remember, your résumé gets scanned in 15–20 seconds.) This format is usually more direct, concise, and focused.

Functional résumés focus on your skills, assets, abilities, accomplishments, and successes, not on how long you have worked at any one place. A functional résumé might indicate that the writer is hiding something, such as previous work experience, re-entry into the marketplace, gaps in employment history, or career transition with no experience in the new career.

Hybrid résumés can also be valuable. This type of résumé combines the Chronological and Functional formats so that you can rearrange your work experience to highlight relevant skills, accomplishments, and successes. You can list employers you have worked with that would be known in the industry. Gaps in employment are not as visible. The Hybrid allows you to point out your strengths and hide your weaknesses.

Third, we'll review some different résumé examples.

Chronological

Some things to consider as you read this résumé (*Sample 2-A*).

- How long did it take you to review the résumé to know what kind of position this person is seeking?

- Does the résumé appear to be organized, succinct, and focused?

- If you had only 15–20 seconds to review this résumé, what parts would stand out in your mind?

- If you were seeking an administrative assistant, would you consider interviewing this candidate?

Functional

Some things to consider as you read this résumé (*Sample 2-B*).

- Does this person's skills impress you?

- Can you make a decision about this résumé in 15-20 seconds?

- Do you find yourself wondering how long this person did those skills and where?

- Were you let down when you found out how old some of the work experience was?

- What are some of the items in this résumé that you would want to incorporate in your résumé?

Hybrid

Chronological/Functional combined (*Sample 2-C*).

Ask yourself the same questions listed above.

Learn from these to build an effective résumé.

Fourth, we'll add action words and list specific skills to spice up your résumé. You will need to set your résumé apart from others by using **action** verbs that paint a clear picture of **your** talents and accomplishments.

For example, rather than saying,

> **Worked** with team to create and produce new corporate intranet site.

Instead, say,

> **Collaborated** and **participated** on team to produce new corporate intranet site.

Use strong verbs to portray your accomplishments and skills. (See Chapter 1 for a sample list of action verbs.)

In addition to using powerful verbs in your résumé, it is equally important to include vital skills. There are two types of skills.

1. Functional skills show an individual's level of ability to relate to other people, data, and equipment/hardware.

2. Self-management skills refer to an individual's ability to govern and conduct himself or herself in an employment setting.

As you create your résumé, refer to the self-management skills list (*Sample 2-D*) and the functional skills list (*Sample 2-E*).

Other Items to Consider

- **Cover Letters**—A cover letter should always accompany your résumé, especially if you mail, email, or fax your résumé. It provides a brief introduction of you and serves as a good starting point. See *Cover Letter Tips*.

- **Electronic Résumé**—To be successful in today's technological market, due to the use of the Internet and Web-based hiring, it is best to have an electronic version of your résumé. See *Tips for Creating an Internet-Ready Résumé.*

- **Do's and Don'ts List**—Double-check everything and do not rely on your word processor's spell and grammar checks; they have been known to be wrong! You have all the time you need before you send out any résumés, so get it right. Make a good first impression.

Sample 2-A
Chronological Résumé

Mary B. Smith

1234 Adams Street

City, State 12345

216-888-1234,

Email: mailme@mail.com

OBJECTIVE

Senior Administrator

SUMMARY OF QUALIFICATIONS

More than ten years of broad-based experience as an administrator in fast-paced, manufacturing environments. Proven track record of successfully managing multiple projects concurrently from concept to delivery with quality work and within time-frame and budget.

PROFESSIONAL EXPERIENCE

XYZ Corporation, Tallahassee, FL (2000 to Present)

Senior Administrator, Corporate Human Resources (1996 to Present)

Provide support to the corporate VP, Human Resources. Manage human resource projects including Variable Pay Plan, HR Customer Survey, Master Bonus System, and Sales Incentive Plan ensuring prompt delivery of time-sensitive materials and meeting all program deadlines. Write and edit monthly HR newsletter and consistently meet publication timelines. Manage the HR Special Awards and Incentives Program promoting team spirit and improving customer service across divisions. Work with interdisciplinary team to produce new HR intranet site. Responsible for keeping all information on the site up-to-date and correct.

Promoted for outstanding performance from HR Division Administrator to Corporate Senior Administrator within eight months.

Administrator (1995 to 2000)

Provided HR support to the Technical Director, including the reduction in workforce due to restructuring. Planned and coordinated major office moves within site facilities for 75-person group.

ABC Corporation, Western Region, Burlingame, CA 1990 to 1995

Personnel Supervisor and Executive Assistant to the President

Managed all personnel function for 65 sales employees. Coordinated all travel arrangements for the sales team. Provided all administrative support for the president including creating presentation materials for key Board of Director and shareholders meetings.

PMN Corporation, Seattle, WA 1985 to 1990

Executive Assistant to the Managing Director

Managed an office of six assistants providing administrative support. Oversaw the installation of the computer network system for the division. Streamlined the tracking of customers by setting up office database system.

EDUCATION

Master of Arts in Human Resource Development
Florida State University, Tallahassee, FL
(Currently in progress, December 20XX)

Bachelor of Arts in English; 1985,
University of Washington, Seattle, WA

ADDITIONAL INFORMATION

- Fluent in Spanish: read, write, and speak
- Traveled and lived overseas
- Excellent skills in Internet and Web page management

Sample 2-B
Functional Résumé

Only U. Gough

1234 Lakeshore Drive

Birmingham, AL 35229

(205) 123-4560

Email: mabailey@gateway.com

QUALIFICATIONS

Self-starter with proven skills in developing and managing systems to improve work flow, office management, supervision, and customer-service relations. Excellent communication skills, proficient in WordPerfect, Microsoft Word, Excel, and Lotus.

MANAGER

Supervised 15 employees, including technical and clerical.

Hired, counseled, and evaluated personnel.

Created employee recognition award program.

Monitored Quality Improvement (QI) processes and facilitated QI improvement meetings; implemented improvement processes, including creating work forms.

Managed the inspection process of more than 700 facilities, including data calculation and analysis, correspondence preparation, and follow-up consultation.

Evaluated and resolved regulatory compliance issues.

Functioned as liaison among regulatory agency, professional owners, managers, service companies, city/county inspectors, contractors, and architects.

Prepared monthly and bimonthly reports, budget, purchase orders, and payroll.

Investigated customer concerns and resolved problems.

COMMUNICATION/TRAINING

Prepared training materials for employees, mangers, and owners.

Conducted training programs for employees, managers, and owners.

Created and edited monthly employee newsletter.

Planned and presented continuing education programs.

Created and coordinated educational/motivational program for inner-city school.

EMPLOYMENT HISTORY

Women's Diagnostic Center (February 2001–June 2003)

Jefferson County Department of Health (February 1997–February 2001)

EDUCATION

Stamford University, Bachelor of Science, Business Administration, 1997

University of Alabama, Associate of Science Birmingham, Paralegal, 1992

COMMUNITY ACTIVITIES AND HONORS

Leader, Stephen Ministry (church laity ministry)

Facilitator, single adult workshops

Dean's List

Sample 2-C
Hybrid Résumé

Ihva Job

32 Main Street

Anywhere, US 12367

(123) 555-4367 Email:money@aal.com

Objective

Seeking position as a Staff Accountant to assist a company in its financial accounting.

Education

Mouse University, School of Business, Orlando, FL

Bachelor's degree in Accounting, May 2010; Minor: Computer Science; Overall GPA 3.6

Professional Skills

Accounting

Successfully completed a two-semester internship at AccuCount, Inc.

Skilled in all areas of accounting, including accounts payable/receivable, and payroll.

Currently taking CPA course.

Awarded "Best Intern," Spring 2008.

Customer Relations

Effectively interact with corporate and small business clients.

Participate in client meetings.

Computer

Skilled in Excel, Lotus, WordPerfect, Word, and other data-based programs.

Familiar with PC and Mac environments.

Employment History

Accounting Intern, AccuCount, Inc., Hometown, FL, 9/2010–5/2012

Worked closely with Lead Payroll Accountant in all daily functions.

Payroll Clerk, Mickey Squeezers, Newtown, FL, 4/2008–8/2010

Assisted in the management of payroll for approximately 75 employees.

Cashier, Mickey Squeezers, Newtown, FL, 6/2007–4/2008

Served as cashier in high-volume, food store.

Activities

Accounting Society, Mouse University—Treasurer, 9/2009–5/2010

Computer Science Club, Mouse University—Member, 1/2009–5/2010

Sample 2-D
Self-Management Skills

A
Adventuresome (ness)
Adept (ness)
Alert (ness)
Assertive (ness)
Astute (ness)
Attention to details
Authentic (ity)
Authority, handles others well
Aware (ness)

B

C
Calm (ness)
Candid (ness)
Challenges, thrives
Character, has fine
Clothes, dresses well
Committed, commitment to growth
Competent (competence)
Concentration
Concerned
Conscientious (ness)
Cooperative (cooperation)
Courage (ous)
Creative, manifests creativity
Curious (curiosity)

D
Dependable
Dependability
Diplomatic
Discreet
Driving (as, in ambition) drive
Dynamic (ness)

E
Easygoing (ness)
Emotional Stability
Empathy (empathetic)
Enthusiastic, enthusiasm
Exceptional
Expert
Experienced
Expressive (ness)

F
Firm (ness)
Flexible (flexibility)

G
Generous, generosity
Gets along well with others

H
High energy level
Honest (y)
Humanly-oriented (warm)

I
Imaginative
Impulses, controls well
Imitating (initiative)
Innovative (innovation)
Insight (ful)
Integrity, displays constant

J
Judgment, has good

K

L
Loyal (ty)

M
Material world, deals well with things

N
Natural (ness)
O
Objective
Open minded (ness)
Optimistic (optimism)
Orderly (orderliness)
Outgoing (ness)
Outstanding
P
Patient (patience)
Penetrating
Perceptive (ness)
Persevering (perseverance)
Persisting (persistence)
Pioneering
Playful (ness)
Poise
Polite (ness)
Precise attainment of set goals
    limits or standards
Punctual (ity)
Q
R
Reliable (reliabilityo
Resourceful (ness)
Responsible (responsibility)
Responsive (ness)
Risk-taking

S
Self-confident (confidence)
Self-control, good
Self-reliant (reliance)
Self-respect
Sense of humor, great
Sensitive (sensitivity)
Sincere (sincerity)
Sophisticated
Spontaneous (spontaneity)
Strikes balance, happy medium
Strong as, under stress
Successful
Sympathetic (sympathy) warm
T
Tactful (ness) Thinks on his/her
    feet
Thorough (ness) Takes nothing for
    granted
Tidy (tidiness)
Time, deals well with being
    punctual (punctuality)
Tolerant (tolerance)
U
Uncommon, Unique
V
Versatile (versatility)
Vigor (ous)
W
X
Y
Z

Sample 2-E
Functional Skills

Functional skills refer to those competencies that enable an individual to relate to people, data, and things in a combination according to some degree of complexity appropriate to his/her level of ability.

PEOPLE (Human beings)	DATA (Information, knowledge, and concepts)	THINGS (Inanimate objects)
Analytical Skills	Administrative Skills	Manual Dexterity
Bargaining Skills	Artistic Skills	Mechanical Skills
Communication Skills	Assessment Skills	Operating
Consulting Skills	Clerical Skills	Controlling Skills
Coordinating Skills	Conceptual Acuity Skills	Precision Skills
Counseling Skills	Design Skills	Setting-Up Skills
Debating Skills	Editing Skills	Working Skills
Decision-Making Skills	Evaluation Skills	
Delegation Skills	Financial Management Skills	
Diplomacy Skills	Fiscal Analysis Skills	
Foreign Language Skills	Forecasting Skills	
Implementing Skills	Imagination Skills	
Interpersonal Skills	Innovation Skills	
Interviewing Skills	Judgmental Skills	
Investigating Skills	Managerial Skills	
Leadership Skills	Mathematical Skills	
Listening Skills	Money-Making Skills	
Negotiation Skills	Musical Skills	
Organizational Skills	Observational Skills	
Perception Skills	Office Skills	
Persuasive Skills	Planning Skills	
Public Relations Skills	Reporting Skills	
Reconciliation Skills	Research Skills	
Sales/Marketing Skills	Synthesizing Skills	
Social Skills	Visual Conception Skills	
Supervisory Skills	Writing Skills	
Teaching Skills		
Training Skills		

Blueprint #2-2
Putting It All Together

MATERIALS NEEDED

Paper and pen

Chair, desk, and light

Information generated for *Blueprint #1-1*

Computer with a word processor

PREP TIME

One (1) hour

DIRECTIONS

- Based on the résumé format you have selected, begin to fill in your information.

- Under "Objective," if you use this header, be general in your statement. You do not want to lose other possible opportunities the company might have.

- Under "Education," include only post high school and advanced degrees, such as a masters, doctorate, and attorney. Non-degree classes are not included in this section.

- Under "Employment," include ALL your employers. Do not leave gaps in your résumé.

- Under each employer include: (a) a brief description of the company, (b) a brief description of your job and responsibilities, and (c) some bullet points for the successes and accomplishments you achieved in your position with that employer.

- Keep your résumé simple: only give the highlights and strong points. Do not go into extreme detail. The employer will not take the time to read your résumé if it is too long or detailed.

- Under other headers, include only the appropriate information needed for the job you are applying for. Some other headers could include:

  A. Other organizations, licenses, and affiliations

  B. Personal

  C. References

- Make sure you do a spell check and proofread for grammar. Read the résumé aloud. Do not assume the spell check will catch everything—it will not!

- Your finished résumé should be on conservative, good quality paper. Use white or off-white paper.

- Be certain it is clean, neat, and presentable. This shows professionalism.

SUMMARY

After you have completed a final copy of your résumé or your "self-portrait," look it over to make sure it accurately portrays you as the prospective employee. Just as you did on the sample résumés, ask yourself these questions:

- Does the résumé appear organized, succinct, and focused?

- If you only had 15–20 seconds to review this résumé, what parts would stand out?

- Is any item unclear or vague?

- Did you use powerful verbs and identify specific skills?

HOMEWORK

Remember the list of the three most important items you listed at the beginning of this chapter for your résumé? Go back and look at the list. Do they still apply? Would you change anything? What have you learned in the process of creating your résumé?

Cover Letter—
An Introduction to Your Résumé

COVER LETTER TIPS

(See *Samples 2-F, 2-G,* and, for fun, see *2-H.*)

- Do not mail a résumé without a cover letter.

- Use a personal salutation to the vice president, director, or manager of personnel or human resources, or the specific name of an executive elsewhere in the company. If no name is known, call to obtain the appropriate title and name.

- Do not use a generic cover letter.

- If sending a copy to the hiring department manager, refer to this action in a letter to the personnel or human resources manager.

- Use paper that matches the résumé (good bond paper). Only use the front side.

- Include telephone numbers and email address in your return address.

- Sign your name legibly and large enough to be easily read. Blue ink is preferred.

- Keep copies of all correspondence.

- Follow-up on résumés sent within three to five days by telephone.

- When faxing or emailing a résumé and cover letter, call to see if the person received them. An original copy may also be mailed with a reference to the fax or email.

- Keep the cover letter short, to the point, three to five paragraphs.

FORMATTING TIPS

- Return mailing address and date at the top of page: left, centered, or right justified.

- Name of person and institution three lines below the date and flush with left margin.

- Single space the body of the letter. Double space between paragraphs.

- Paragraphs may begin at the left margin or five spaces to the right.

- Type the complimentary close two lines below the last line of the letter.

- Type your name four lines below the complimentary close.

- Sign your name on the cover letter above your typed name.

- Type "Enclosure," if needed, two lines below your typed name.

LETTER CONTENT

PARAGRAPH # 1—Interest

Get the person's attention by introducing yourself and letting the employer know why you are writing and possibly how you learned of the position or the company. This should create some interest in you. Give your current status as a student or an employee. Be sure to mention any person the reader might know who also knows you. Recommend that the employer contact the person who knows you, your skills, and can speak positively about you.

PARAGRAPH # 2—Sell

Offer your services. Mention one or two qualifications you think would be of greatest interest to the employer, addressing your remarks to his or her point of view. Draw attention to your strongest points, but do not rewrite your résumé in this paragraph. You must convince the reader that you have something beneficial to offer. What can you do for the employer? Why should this person take his/her time to speak with you? Why are you qualified? Why are you a good candidate for the position?

PARAGRAPH # 3—Action

A "call for action." Be certain your closing statement is positive and makes a request for a specific action from the reader. Let the reader know that you will be following-up with a telephone call. Close your sale. If writing to a local employer, the third paragraph should ask for an interview and say you will call within the next three to four days to set an appointment time. If you are writing to an out-of-town employer, you could say, "I plan to visit Atlanta the week of May 7–14 and would welcome the opportunity to meet with you personally." Show appreciation to the reader for his/her time and consideration.

Sample 2-F
Cover Letter—Responding to an Ad

Joseph B. Smith
777 Moriah Lane
Niceville, State 32165
(565) 988-7676
Email: jbs@ubu.com

September 30, 20XX

Mr. Jackson, Director of Human Resources
Parker & Associates
524 Fairview Lane
Any City, State 35401

Dear Mr. Jackson:

In response to your recent newspaper advertisement for the *Vice President of Sales and Marketing* position, please accept this letter as my formal application. Enclosed is my résumé showing my education, experience, and background credentials, along with specific successes and accomplishments.

I have more than 10 years experience in the sales and marketing field, and 6 years experience as a manager. Throughout my career, I have won top sales awards. I have hired and trained other sales representatives on specific sales techniques to increase their sales. I also enjoy working with the public, and also demonstrating products and educating others.

I believe I would excel in your position because I truly find sales and marketing a challenging and rewarding career. Additionally, my personal background in sales offers an advantage in understanding the sales representatives' needs and how to motivate them.

I would like to arrange an interview to discuss my qualifications and how I can assist your company. I am available for an interview at a convenient time.

Thank you in advance for your time and consideration.

Sincerely,

Joseph B. Smith

Enclosure

Sample 2-G
Cover Letter—Unsolicited

Joseph B. Smith
777 Moriah Lane
Niceville, State 32165
(565) 988-7676
Email: jbs@ubu.com

September 30, 20XX

Mr. Jackson, Director of Human Resources
Parker & Associates
524 Fairview Lane
Any City, State 35401

Dear Mr. Jackson:

I am sending you this letter to introduce myself to your company. I have a strong background in *Sales and Marketing* to resort communities. Enclosed is my résumé showing my education, experience, and background credentials, along with specific successes and accomplishments.

I have more than ten years experience in the sales and marketing field, and six years of direct experience as a manager.

Throughout my sales and marketing career, I have won top sales awards. I have hired and trained other sales representatives on specific sales techniques to increase their sales. I enjoy working with the public and also demonstrating products and educating others. I believe I would excel in your company because I truly find sales and marketing a challenging and rewarding career. Additionally, my personal selling background offers an advantage in understanding the sales representatives' needs and how to motivate them.

I would like to arrange an interview to discuss my qualifications and how I could assist your company. I am available for an interview at a convenient time.

Thank you in advance for your time and consideration.

Sincerely,

Joseph B. Smith

Enclosure

Sample 2-H
Just for Fun!

To Whom It May Concern:

Enclosed for consideration is a copy of my résumé. I hope this letter will answer any questions you might have about my job history. I bring a variety of experience and would welcome an interview. For the reasons listed below, these jobs just were not me.

1. My first job was working in an orange juice factory, but I got canned—couldn't concentrate.

2. Then I worked in the woods as a lumberjack, but I just couldn't hack it, so they gave me the ax.

3. After that I tried to be a tailor, but I just wasn't suited for it, mainly because it was a so-so job.

4. Next, I tried working in a muffler factory, but that was too exhausting, and I kept on backfiring.

5. I tried to be a barber, but I just couldn't cut it.

6. Then I tried to be a chef—figured it would add a little spice to my life, but I just didn't have the thyme.

7. I attempted to be a deli worker, but any way I sliced it, I couldn't cut the mustard. My best job was being a musician, but eventually I found I wasn't noteworthy.

8. I studied a long time to become a doctor, but I didn't have any patience. Next was a job in a shoe factory. I tried, but I just didn't fit in.

9. I became a professional fisherman, but discovered that I couldn't live on my net income.

10. I managed to get a good job working for a pool maintenance company, but the work was just too draining.

11. I got a job at a zoo feeding giraffes, but I was fired because I wasn't up to it.

12. So then I got a job in a work-out center, but they said I wasn't fit for the job.

13. After many years of trying to find steady work, I finally got a job as a historian until I realized there was no future in it.

14. My last job was working at Starbucks, but I had to quit because it was always the same old grind.

I look forward to hearing from you.

Sincerely Insecure,

Ined A. Job

Tips for Creating an Internet-Ready Résumé

An Internet version of your résumé is necessary for today's business environment. If you are looking for a job and you would like to (or you need to) submit an electronic résumé, there are a variety of ways to use an Internet-ready version of your résumé. You might choose to create:

- A text-formatted document that can be scanned

- A résumé to paste into an email

- A résumé that is submitted directly to a résumé database using a Web-based form

Creating a Multipurpose Résumé

- Review your computer-generated résumé for spelling, grammatical, and/or punctuation errors.

- Save the document by clicking "SAVE AS" from the file menu in your software program.

- Rename your file by adding ".TXT" to the filename and selecting file type "Text Only" or "ASCII."

- Save and close your file.

- A dialog box might appear telling you that you will lose formatting by saving your document as a text file.

- Click "yes" to confirm that you want to save as text.

- Open your saved text file in a text editor such as WordPad for the PC or Simple Text for Macintosh.

- All formatting, such as italics, will be gone. The text document will be left justified.

Useful Tips

- Each line should be no longer than 60 characters (including spaces).

- Font size should be 10 or 12 point.

- Always indicate the end of each line by hitting the "Return" or "Enter" key.

- Create spaces by using the space bar.

- Highlight different sections of your résumé by using a "+" or "*."

- **Note:** Résumé databases do not recognize bullets.

- Emphasize information by capitalizing rather than bolding words in your résumé.

- Always check your final version by copying and pasting into the body of an email message and sending it to a friend or to yourself!

- Your e-résumé is now ready to submit.

Some Internet Sites to Consider—A Few Are FREE

www.CareerBuilder.com

www.Monster.com

www.Employment911.com

www.6FigureJobs.com

Many, many more are available. The easiest and fastest way to find sites to which you can submit your résumé is to do a keyword search on the Internet. Type in "résumé," and you'll find a list of sites to "surf" for hours.

CHAPTER 3—MAKING CONTACTS

Getting the Interview

Introduction

Common sense tells us that first impressions do make a difference when interviewing for a job. Unfortunately, some people do not use common sense. According to a survey of personnel executives, potential job candidates can do the strangest things.

When I asked a job applicant about his hobbies, he stood up and started tap dancing around my office. One interviewee said he was so well qualified that if he didn't get the job, it would prove that the company's management was incompetent. An applicant listed his mother as a reference. When called, she said, "I wouldn't hire him; he's not very dependable."

Networking: The Link to Credibility

Networking is a valuable tool in getting an interview. It puts you in contact with the right person, and the referral gives you credibility. Not quite sure how to network? Do you think you don't know the right people? Don't let the lack of knowledge slow you down.

Blueprint #3-1
Getting the Interview

MATERIALS NEEDED

Paper and pen

Quiet place

Contact Worksheet (*Sample 3-B*)

Personal/Professional Contacts (*Sample 3-C*)

Telephone

Confidence

Your Résumé (Chapter 2)

PREP TIME

Four (4) hours to as much time as you want to learn

DIRECTIONS

- Find a quiet place to begin this exercise.

- **Professional Contacts**—Search your memory for every possible contact you have or have had in non-personal relationships and make a detailed list of those contacts (*Sample 3-C*).

- **Personal Contacts**—Search your memory for every possible contact you have or have had in non-professional relationships and make a detailed list of those contacts (*Sample 3-C*).

- Begin to call each contact you have written down on your lists (*Sample 3-B*).

- Tell the contact that you have begun a search for new employment opportunities and called to ask for his/her help and assistance. (*Sample 3-A*)

- Based on your résumé, give a very brief overview of your background and the type of position you are seeking.

- This step is extremely important. The contact needs to clearly understand the type of job you are seeking. *Do not* leave it up to the contact to know what would or would not be the right career/job opportunity for you.

- Try to get three to five referral names from each contact you speak with. These referrals, when contacted, should also give you additional leads to pursue. When contacting a person to whom you were referred, always use the contact's name. It establishes instant credibility and creates a bond with that contact right away. This person is now more likely not only to take your call right away, but he/she will take your request for help more seriously than they would from someone they don't know.

- When you do get through to someone who has a hiring need, try to get the interview or a face-to-face meeting as soon as possible. Ask open-ended questions and try to avoid yes or no questions. An example would be, "Would one day this week or next week be better for us to get together?"

- If the contact doesn't have a hiring need, ask if you can meet with them anyway to get his/her advice on the types of jobs that exist in that particular industry, or even to get advice on your job search. It is a good ego boost to the person to know that his/her advice would be valuable, and most times people do like to help.

- Try to get the face-to-face meeting; this is how you get hired!

- See the section about marketing through the "Use of Social Media in Career Search" later in this chapter.

SUMMARY

The purpose of networking is to expand your contact base through people and the use of social media. The more contacts you develop through networking, the higher the probability of obtaining meaningful interviews. Do not be shy in asking for referrals, as you never know who can help you. Be clear and direct in describing what you are seeking for yourself. This will assist the contact in being able to understand whom to refer you to.

The time spent networking does and will produce interviews that might not otherwise be obtained. When you use a referral's name, it adds instant credibility to getting through to your contact. You will be tapping into the "hidden job market" if you use this method to obtain interviews. So take the time, be bold, and keep a log of every contact, call, and the results.

Exactly as I planned, it will happen. Following my blueprints, it will take shape. Who could ever cancel such plans? His is the hand that's reached out. Who could brush it aside?

—Isaiah 14: 24, 27

HOMEWORK

Not quite sure what to say when you call your contacts? Refer to the Networking Script (*Sample 3-A*). Read it and get familiar with it. Remember first impressions? This will truly be your first impression, but over the phone. So how you sound is just as important as how you appear.

TIPS

In networking, it is important to fully maximize the potential of each contact. Each contact you make can either be one less contact remaining on your list, or perhaps two or three more names added to your list.

With increased names, the pressure of making the "right" contact is lessened. Adversely, by watching your contact list being reduced before your very eyes, the level of anxiety increases as you near the final unsuccessful attempt to get a job! Which position would you rather find yourself in?

Rule of Thumb

Control the controllable! Increase your network with every contact, and eventually you might have to decide which job offer you want to accept. And that is a good problem to have.

No contact or phone calls = no job offers! This is the law of averages: the more calls you make, the greater the probability of obtaining successful results. *Stay the Course.*

Sample 3-A
Networking Script

Speaking with Receptionist

You: Hello, this is *(Your Name)*. May I speak with *(Referral's Name)***?**

Receptionist: Why do you want to speak with_____?

You: I was referred to *(Referral's Name)* by a mutual friend.

Receptionist: Yes, and why do you want to speak with_____?

You: I called to ask for *(Referral's Name)* help. [Then, without pause—] *(Person who gave referral)* suggested he/she might be able to help me with a project I'm working on. [Keep talking, do not stop.] I'm not selling anything; I just need *(Referral's Name)* assistance and would appreciate speaking with him/her.

Message via Voicemail or Receptionist

You: Hello, *(Person's Name)*, my name is *(Your Name)*. *(Referring person)* referred me to you. My phone number is_____. He/she suggested that you might be able to give me some assistance and help with a project I am working on. When you get a moment today, will you call me back? I only need a few minutes of your time. Again, my phone number is: *(Daytime #)*, and my name is *(First and Last Name)*. I look forward to speaking with you, Goodbye.

Note: It might sound a little cheesy to you, but remember, most people want to help others. If you sound sincere on the recording, your referral will usually return the call. The other reason they will return the call to you is based on their personal integrity—someone dropped their name to you as a valuable, contact person.

Referral Is Available

You: Hello, *(Person's Name)*, my name is *(Your Name)*. *(Referring person)* referred me to you. He/she suggested that I ask for your help. Do you have a few moments to talk?

If Yes: (Very briefly give an explanation of why you called, using either the indirect or direct approach listed below.)

If No: When is a better time to call back? If you prefer to call me, my phone is _____.

Indirect Approach

I am looking for a position as a (*Position*), and (*Referring Person*) suggested that you might know of someone looking for a person with my background. Could you refer me to someone?

Direct Approach

I am seeking a position as a (*Position*), and (*Referring Person*) suggested that you would be the person to talk to. (*Wait for answer.*) Is this a good time to talk?

If Yes: (Give a brief bulleted synopsis of your background, but take less than two minutes. Finally, ask for an interview.) Can we get together in person to discuss how I could be of assistance to your company? (Do not be shy. Be assertive. Ask!)

If No: When is a good time to call back? If you prefer to call me, my phone is _____.

Note: The idea is to get a face-to-face interview. The rule here is that you have to ask for what you want. A second rule is this: the telephone is primarily used for scheduling appointments. Rarely does anyone get a job offer on the phone, prior to a face-to-face meeting.

Be cordial and appreciative. If your referral doesn't have an opening, ask if he/she could suggest someone else to contact. If no specific names are given, ask if there are companies that might be able to use your talents, or any other advice this person might be able to give you.

Sample 3-B
Contact Worksheet

Name	Phone/email	Referral	Notes

Sample 3-C
Personal/Professional Contacts

Date	Name of Person	Company Name	Phone Number
Referred By		Email Address	
Notes			
Date	Name of Person	Company Name	Phone Number
Referred By		Email Address	
Notes			
Date	Name of Person	Company Name	Phone Number
Referred By		Email Address	
Notes			

Use of Social Media in Career Search

IMPORTANCE OF SOCIAL MEDIA IN THE CORPORATE WORLD

Searching for job openings through social media is an art not everyone is aware of how to master. Also, it has been observed that for a career search, job seekers tend to stick to the old, ineffective, traditional ways rather than using the latest trending social media through the Internet.

One explanation for this phenomenon could be that there is a "not-so-true" widespread idea that the corporate community is a closed society of hardcore business species having no similarity at all with the life of a normal human.

Consequently they are perceived as psychologically distant and unapproachable, except for the traditional textbook way defined by them (that is, emails, mails, walk-in interviews, etc.), which in reality is not the only absolute way to communicate with the corporate companies.

PROBLEMS FACED BY JOB SEEKERS

Following are some major problems faced by career job seekers today:

- Increasing global phenomenon of unemployment, where there is an increasing number of jobless people applying for proportionately fewer vacant jobs.

- A big clutter of similar candidates, CVs, and even applying methods, making it extremely difficult for an applicant to stand out from the rest of the crowd. All this even makes it difficult for the employers to filter good and bad candidates.

- Human psyche of resistance to change, where job seekers are not adapting and adjusting to the latest social media trends of career search and thus not utilizing the full potential of the growing relationship between careers and social media.

- Fear of failure in spending time and banking on the social media for a successful career search.

A Few Important Guidelines

In the context of a career search, a job seeker must be aware of the following useful guidelines about the corporate world, career opportunities, and the relation to trending social media. All these guidelines will help the career candidate in minimizing and overcoming many of the problems mentioned earlier.

Job seekers must realize that corporate companies and their professionals are actively present on different facets of the social media, such as LinkedIn, Facebook, Twitter, Viadeo, and Xing.

Most of the top companies also announce job vacancies on their social media pages. The example below is of Unilever career opportunities posted on LinkedIn.

In fact, many companies in developed nations have now opted to use their social media accounts for recruitment purposes. As per research, more than 70 percent of European companies have a presence on social media sites, and the most relevant business function being utilized by these companies is of the HR department, specifically of the recruitment task (Jörgen Sundberg, 2014).

A hybrid action plan by the job seeker, that is, reaching the company through social media **and** traditional methods (emails, walk-in interviews, mailed résumés) is always a good idea.

List of Social Media for Career Search

- LinkedIn

- Facebook

- Indeed

- Viadeo

- Xing

- Twitter

For creative career search, LinkedIn tops the list of all social media platforms as being more relevant with recruitment and professional business networking. It is followed by Viadeo and Xing, which compete with LinkedIn on the same lines for being a social media network for corporate gentry. At the same time, almost everyone (whether corporate or non-corporate) is discoverable and reachable on Facebook and Twitter. Indeed is a platform that doesn't allow full-scale professional networking, but it has proven to be a fierce competitor and market penetrator in recent months.

According to the Global Talent Acquisition Monitor, a large scale international research executed by Intelligence Group in 45 countries depicts the following:

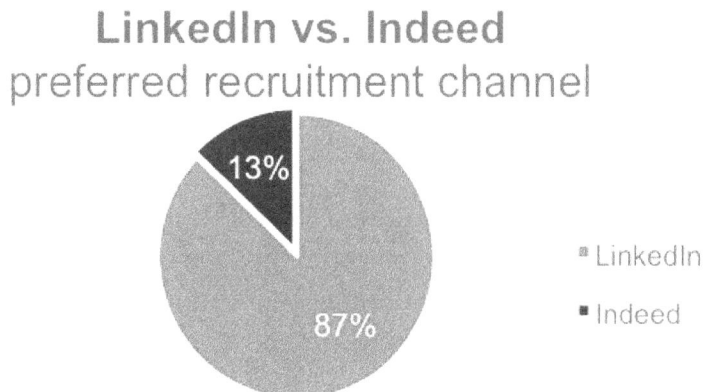

—Recruiting Intelligence, Recruiting Community, 2014

From region to region, preferences of recruitment are different; LinkedIn is mostly dominant worldwide, but in some markets (such as the Netherlands and Japan) Indeed stands at the top. German and Austrian markets are spearheaded by Xing. LinkedIn, slowly and gradually is losing its market share to other direct and indirect competitors.

As a job applicant who is still seeking a career opportunity, you must create your account on all of the mentioned job-seeking, social media portals.

How to Create an Effective LinkedIn Profile

Go to the website www.linkedin.com and signup.

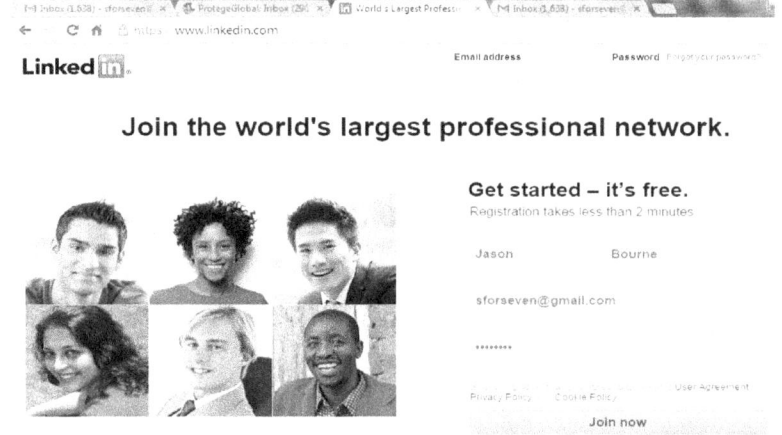

Verify your email address via your mailbox.

Enter some general information regarding yourself and click on "Create My Profile."

Next, LinkedIn will prompt you to enter your email address again so that it can import contacts from your mailbox. **It is strongly advised to skip this step**, because your contacts and prospective employers should only see your profile once it is 100 percent ready for display. Remember, first impression is the last impression.

Therefore, skip this step. You can always do this later. Just think in terms of marketing a product before it is ready. You don't want to do it!

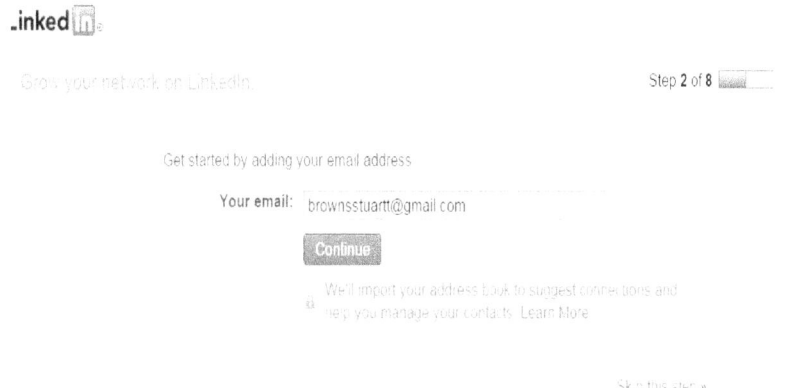

The next screen will ask you a similar question: "Do You Know These People?"

This step should be skipped for the same reason mentioned above.

Next, you will be asked to choose either the free or the premium paid version. Obviously the premium version has its own special benefits, especially the feature that allows a premium user to send a message to anyone whether he/she is in your friend/contact list or not. For job seekers its main usage is to contact professionals/HR departments, and officials who are not on your contact list. Contacting/messaging anyone within your contact list is free without any limits except that you become a spammer. ☺

Your profile-building process has just started. The profile strength meter will give you a fair idea regarding how complete your profile is.

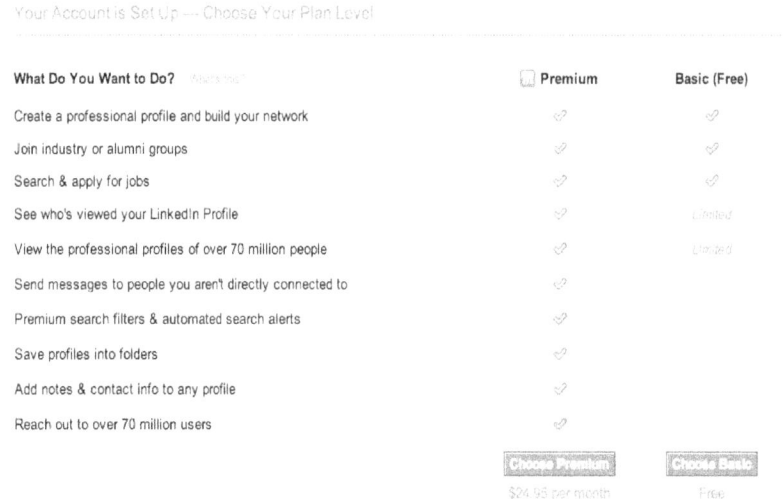

Profile Strength

Intermediate

Jason, keep up with relevant opportunities at Catlin

The main areas of your profile that need to be comprehensively completed are as follows;

- Main Display Details

- Education

- Experience

- Contact Information

- Connections

- Profile Photo

- Background Photo

- Endorsement

MAIN DISPLAY DETAILS

No matter if you are an experienced professional or a recent graduate, this main display is your first impression. It is your "pick-up line" to prospect employers and therefore it should create an impact. Use of industry-specific buzz words in this area and also in your profile is always a wise idea, as companies searching social media sites have software applications looking for these specific "keywords" to locate you. They do not read all the résumés!

This area is customizable and the details should reflect that you are a sought-after creative individual—better than other choices available in the market. Catchy phrases regarding present job or educational background are a must. It is your elevator pitch.

ELEVATOR PITCH

The concept of an elevator pitch is all about an introductory conversation between two strangers, perhaps waiting for an elevator in a corporate plaza. It's a simple way of telling someone about your career as a marketing professional. You can say, "'Hi. I am ABC and I work as a marketing executive for XYZ Company on the fifth floor."

On the other hand, a more creative way would be to say, "Hi. I am ABC and I work for XYZ Company on the fifth floor. Mainly I am responsible for formulating and controlling the marketing efforts of our company and at the same time presenting new profitable opportunities to the board members. In addition, I solve complex client problems as a part and parcel of my daily work routine."

That's it. These three to four sentences are your elevator pitch, which is more than enough for the other person to be intrigued about you and your work and you might get a contact call very soon. The point is, it is all about presenting/branding yourself differently than every other common person in the market.

Note: The elevator-pitch technique could also be used for situations other than the elevator waiting area; think of parties and social gatherings or anywhere people gather.

EDUCATION

In this area you list your academic qualifications in a descending chronological order, that is latest major qualifications / certifications / degrees first, followed by older ones. LinkedIn provides a mechanism of tagging or finding your educational institution from its list. If your institution is available, please make sure you tag it. The same goes for your degree name and specialization.

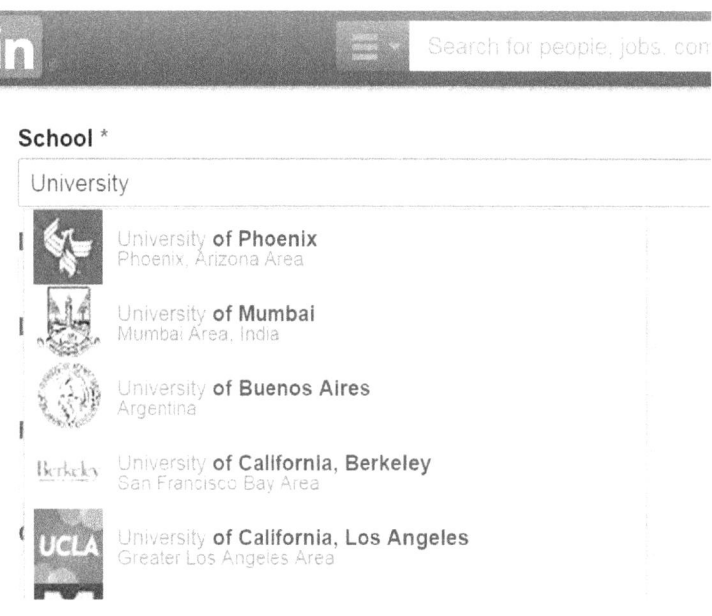

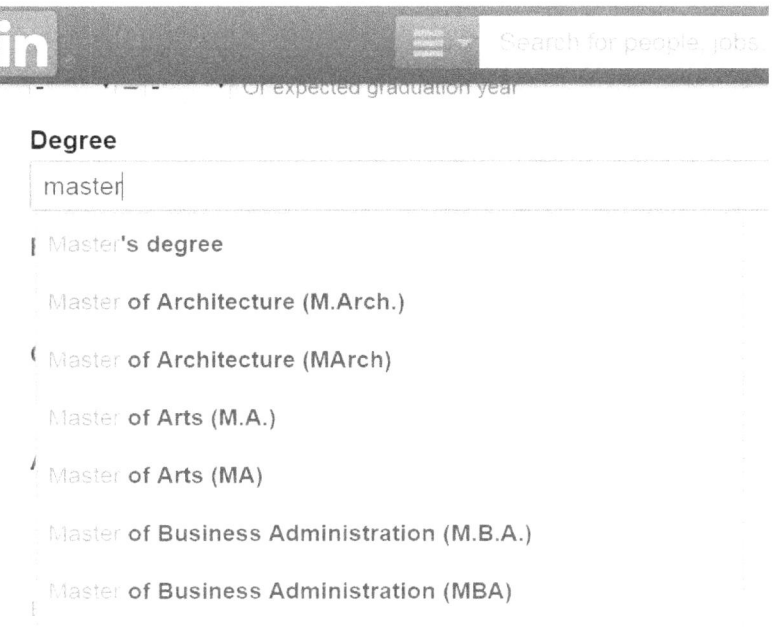

EXPERIENCE

Experience (if any) is also to be added in a similar chronological order, that is, out of all the professional job experiences, the latest ones should come first. When citing your experience of a particular job position, same precautions are to be taken—it should be a synopsis of your performance and responsibilities rather than a complete story line, because remember details are for the interview, not for the résumé. Also, be vigilant when inputting the time period of the job position because the prospective employer might ask for verification references/documents. Try to avoid general statements when citing achievements, such as "improved sales performance," "improved efficiency," etc. It's better to attach a realistic figure to your achievements, such as "improved performance by 40 percent," or "increased revenue turnover by $5 million."

CONTACT INFO

In this section, you can enter your primary email address, contact number, IM/Skype ID, present address.

Also, there is an option to enter your Twitter account URL and links to other social media networks. Cross-linking social media profiles is a good thing, as long as your profiles (such as Facebook, Twitter, etc.) have strict privacy control settings. At the same time be sure that you don't have a loud cover/profile picture, because your main aim is to convince the prospective employer because of your professional/academic skills, rather than your personal-life attributes. Cross-linking a loud Facebook profile can backfire and could result in instant rejection by the prospective employer.

Additionally, at the last screen in this profile section, you'll find your own profile's URL. It is a link that will direct the Web surfer directly to your profile. During the job search, it is highly advised that all your social media profiles are kept as decent and professional as possible, including your Facebook profile.

PROFILE PHOTO AND BACKGROUND PHOTO

It is encouraged to put a professional, nice-looking profile photo, that is upright, smiling, professional, moderately zoomed picture (that displays the upper half of the body) in formal attire.

A background photo could be anything, except something that undermines your profile picture. A good background photo would be one that reflects creativity and complements your primary profile picture.

ADDITIONAL INFO

In this section, you can list your hobbies, interests, and extracurricular activities. Make sure that they captivate the reader. Do not list information mediums or common interests, such as reading books , watching TV , listening to radio, etc. Rather enunciate on specialties, such as interested in political science, alternative medicine, extraterrestrials, nuclear science, documentaries on science and technology, etc.

SKILLS AND ENDORSEMENTS SECTION

In this section you can add different skills you have. There is virtually no limit of adding skill sets, however it is highly recommended that only relevant skills be added. Those skills that are further verified by your connections are perceived to be of more value among profile viewers/prospect employers.

Top Skills

13 Team Management

15 Teamwork

12 Market Research

11 Teaching

9 Team Leadership

6 Negotiation

4 Business Planning

3 Time Management

2 Marketing

RECOMMENDATIONS

Skill endorsements are useful but the real credibility in the eyes of employers is created by recommendations that are given by the people who really know you and are also LinkedIn users. Make sure you have a minimum of five to seven recommendations enhancing your integrity on LinkedIn.

Mark Davitt
Board Member at ACA Education Foundation

Creative and proactive, John consistently demonstrates his talents for projecting a positive public image for our trade association. John's initiative is a true asset.

David Cherner
Legislative Director at Rels Valuation

Working with John at ACA was a tremendous learning experience. John understands the nuances of public relations and always strives to develop cutting edge PR tactics and be forward looking. If innovation and creativity is what you are looking for, John is it.

Mark Neeb
President at The Affiliated Group

I've worked with John for the past two years in my capacity as VP of ACA International, the leading trade association in the credit and collection industry. I can't overstate the importance of John's position at ACA and have been impressed by his foresight in guiding the associations PR efforts. John is a true professional and a pleasure to work with.

Lance Black
President, Northland Group Inc.

The ACA International has found a gem in John Nemo. John is Enthusiastic, organized and very creative. He has found success as Public Relations Director by updating the approach to the positive initiatives the ACA is undertaking. His use of Youtube and the internet champagnes are just the beginning of a well thought out drive for a brighter light on our industry.

JOBS

This section shows jobs available primarily in your region. You can apply for jobs via LinkedIn from this area.

INTERESTS

In this section, you can join and follow various interest groups and companies and also get access to academic networking.

CONNECTIONS

In this section you can add connections/friends/contacts in various ways. You can also find your alumni friends from educational institutions.

Last, but not the least, link-up your mailbox contacts here (the part that was skipped earlier during the beginning phase) and keep adding useful connections that might help you in your job search.

Note: Creating a clutter of unwanted connections is not advised, as this will bring unwanted newsfeeds to your homepage. For the same purpose you can avoid close friends too because friendship and business rarely go together.

WHO'S VIEWED YOUR PROFILE?

An intriguing area highlights the name of those LinkedIn users who viewed your profile in the past two to four weeks. A free-LinkedIn user can see limited names whereas a premium user can see the names of all individuals who viewed his/her profile in past month.

As a job seeker, if you applied to any XYZ company and the HR person of that XYZ company views your profile, you can confirm it from this section. This indicates that the prospective employer is looking into your background and could be interested in considering you.

STRATEGY ONCE YOUR PROFILE IS ON LINKEDIN

After your LinkedIn profile is ready—experience, education, endorsements, recommendations—you can formulate realistic targets, which are neither too high that you can't reach, nor too low that you might easily obtain.

Following are some guidelines:

Set your career search as clearly as possible. Start with the industry you would want to work in, for example, FMCG, BPO, pharmaceutical, financial markets, banking, IT, etc. Choose an industry first.

Select the top five companies in the industry you want to work with and will consider as a career job.

Search those companies on LinkedIn and follow them, if any job opportunities become available, apply via LinkedIn.

If not, then try to find out if any of your friends/acquaintances work in any of these top five companies. I am sure you will find someone. Ask that person for the details of the HR department, that is, how the recruiting is done, who are the "gatekeeper" individuals and who are the right individuals to meet with. **Gatekeepers** are individuals who will not let you meet the right person directly. Keep detailed notes about this information to refer to.

One you know the name of relevant HR personnel, find them on LinkedIn and add them as connections. If they accept your request, that's great! Start a conversation that you would like to know more about available opportunities.

Try to develop a favorable rapport by finding **commonalities.** This includes the possibility that you and the HR person graduated from the same institution, studied from the same faculty, have mutual friends on Facebook or elsewhere, or share a common LinkedIn group. Use this as a common ground, as it is an effective way in breaking the ice to meet someone.

Once you have established a favorable rapport, continue to apply for suitable positions within that company. Even if a vacancy is not available at the moment, stay in touch with the HR person, and in the future you will surely be able to be rewarded from this relationship.

Do this same exercise for all five companies that you listed. And if you're really adventurous, do it for as many companies as possible.

WORDS OF CAUTION

There are no absolutes in this method. Use social media networking with other routine ways for your career job search.

If you are already employed and seeking a new job, do not use your current employer's resources, that is workplace Internet, computers, phones, mail, etc. They are always traceable. Also, do not discuss your job search with anyone in your current company. Keep it confidential from your current boss.

Do not leave any tracks on social media regarding your job search. In that case, set your supervisor and sensitive contacts to privacy control lists.

Make sure your social media sites do not have anything negative or controversial on them (from you or any of your friends). Many people have been fired from their jobs due to that. Include only one personal photo on your social media sites. You don't want to be discriminated against because of hair style, facial hair, or other things that could keep you from getting an interview. You want to get interviews because of your talents, skills, experiences, knowledge, and abilities to perform in the career job.

Also make your personal social media pages as decent and moderate as possible. In a nutshell, keep your personal social media and your professional networking fully separate from each other, but realize that anyone could view your sites at any time.

Hiring managers might initially spend only 20 or 30 seconds reviewing your application, so extra pages are either ignored or they dilute the impact of the others. Your résumé should be for highlights, not extensive detail. The extensive detail comes in the face-to-face interview.

Consider your social media pages as a marketing brochure. Tell the readers just enough to create the "I want to speak with that person" reaction. Remember, you are a product, so market yourself that way. Once you have the interview opportunity, this is where you have to "sell" yourself about your value to the employer.

Use your elevator pitch wherever possible.

Use a thank-you note. In today's competitive job market, sending a well formulated thank-you note can be the difference between getting the job and being completely disregarded. According to research, almost three-fourths of job seekers never send a thank-you note. In a thank-you note, you can always reiterate your achievements, supplement your interview answers, share ideas, and be proactive. Use the actual mail service with a postage stamp, do not email your thank-you note.

Try to create a holistic blend of academics, interests, professional experience, and the position applied for. Anything that's an obstacle to this holistic blend, should be removed from your résumé.

Use power phrases in your online profile, rather than apologetic phrases. If you need further explanation, search online with the words "power phrases" for more details.

The following example would clarify the concept of holistic blending:

A friend of mine completed his ACCA (**Association of Chartered Certified Accountants**) which is a finance/audit-related degree. Later, he took a complete U-turn and decided to pursue a career in **F**ast-**M**oving **C**onsumer **G**oods (FMCG) or **C**onsumer **P**ackaged **G**oods (CPG) marketing specifically on the branding side. He completed his one-year marketing program from a UK university. After completion of his degree, he got a job in the operations department of a **B**usiness **P**rocess **O**utsourcing (BPO) company. He kept searching for a marketing (branding) job and during his job search, he never mentioned ACCA in his CV/résumé nor the operations department job in the BPO company, because both were contradictory with his future goal of a career in a brand department job within a top FMCG company.

Also in his CV, his interests and hobbies were those that were brand/advertising/FMCG related and at the same time he aligned his personality with his ambition, that is, owning the latest iPhone, wearing expensive branded attire, and eventually he found a career job in one of the top FMCG companies. So the whole crux of this story is that your personality, goals, interests, and hobbies in your CV should align with the position you're applying for, meaning they should all blend. Anything that is not directly related should be removed from the CV/résumé. It is better to have a fresh graduate CV than to have a contradicting CV.

FINAL WORDS FOR THIS CHAPTER

Your career search on social media should definitely start with LinkedIn, but that's just the beginning. Contacting relevant HR personnel on Facebook, Twitter, and Google Plus is always a good idea, as long as you are not being aggressive with your efforts. You have to identify this fine line between energy and aggression, for example, **do** contact HR officials of different companies over the social media but **do not** make their social media experience miserable by spamming routine messages to them. Allow them distance and exclusivity and at the same time sneak in with your application. Try to influence them with your gentleness and creativity and cash-in your favorable rapport in getting the opportunity before it is advertised to the masses.

Once you have completed your profile on LinkedIn, you can do create profiles for Xing Viadeo, and Indeed. These networks are similar to LinkedIn. They are just another route to the same destination, and possibly they could give better results than LinkedIn—you never know. Finally, whatever do's and don'ts apply to hard-copy résumés, the same also apply for your résumés/profiles on social media.

SUMMARY OF THE STEPS OUTLINED

Create a decent, professional profile on all mainstream social media networks, especially those that are trendy in your geographical area (LinkedIn, Facebook, Twitter, Xing, Viadeo, Indeed, etc.).

Make sure you maintain decorum and discipline in all your profiles across all social media platforms.

Do not add any contacts unless and until your profile is ready for marketing/display.

Clearly define your career search goal, that is, any five favorite companies you really want to work for.

Find those five companies on LinkedIn and other social media platforms and try to approach them. If not found on social media, then try to find any acquaintance and use him/her as a bridge to reach them.

Identify "gatekeepers" so that in your next attempt, you can try to bypass them

Do not forget to incorporate the strategy of "holistic blending" and "elevator pitch" in your first and ongoing correspondences with your favorite companies.

Maintain your self-esteem and energy by using more "power phrases" and avoid apologetic phrases in your profile and in any form of communication with the targeted company.

Keep trying different social media platforms for your favorite companies and you might get a chance for a vacancy before it is publicly advertised. Even if public ads are placed, with all your efforts you will have a favorable rapport as compared to new applicants. Trying social media is an altogether "nothing to lose" strategy.

Along with perusing social media in your job search, keep utilizing the traditional methods. A hybrid always has more chances of success than an absolute one-sided approach.

References

Recruiting Intelligence, Recruiting Community. (2014). Retrieved from http://www.ere.net/2014/11/27/the-battle-for-global-recruiting-domination-indeed-vs-linkedin/.

Sundberg, J. (2014). *Link Humans.* Retrieved from http://linkhumans.com/blog/social-recruiting-europe.

Blueprint #3-2
Preparing for the Interview

MATERIALS NEEDED

Company information

Pad (paper) and pen

Questions to Ask (*Sample 3-D*)

Freshly pressed clothes, proper attire

Map with driving directions

Positive attitude

PREP TIME

Three (3) to four (4) hours

DIRECTIONS

- Do your homework about the company that will be interviewing you. Get as much information as possible, such as business activity, products, services, etc.

- From this company information, develop a list of questions that you want to ask (*Sample 3-D*).

- Review possible questions that you could be asked (*Sample 3-E*).

- Practice, practice, practice. Be prepared; know your strengths and weaknesses if and when asked (Chapter 1).

- Make a practice drive, if local, to the company to see how long it takes or if there are any detours. Check out where you need to park. DO NOT BE LATE.

- The night before, pick out the clothes you intend to wear. Be certain that they are clean and freshly pressed.

- Check your attitude, practice turning it up to HIGH. Be positive, friendly, and courteous.

SUMMARY

Do your homework about the company that you will be interviewing with, as it could make the difference between losing or winning the job. Professional athletes do their homework; they watch films of their competition and study how and what they do. If you are properly prepared, the interview will go well.

Ask your spouse or a friend to assist you in asking practice questions of you (*Sample 3-E*). It is easier to know what you are going to say before you're asked. The person unprepared might answer the question with, "That's a good question." Don't be caught unprepared; be a professional; do your homework and *practice, practice, practice*.

> *Call to me and I will answer you. I'll tell you marvelous and wondrous things that you could never figure out on your own.*

—Jeremiah 33:3

HOMEWORK

Ask yourself the following questions:

- If I were the interviewer, what questions would I ask?

- What would I like to know about a job candidate?

- What would I want the candidate to know about the job?

- Would I hire ME?

- Why?

NOTES

_____

_____

_____

_____

_____

_____

_____

Be patient with yourself. Self-growth is tender; it's holy ground.
There's no greater investment.

—Stephen Covey

Sample 3-D
Questions to Ask

About the Company/Position

Questions should be prewritten on a pad that you take to the interview.

- Is this a newly created position? Or is there an incumbent in the position?

- Why is there a need for this position?

- Where has the incumbent or previous person in this position come up short?

- Could you please elaborate as to responsibilities, experiences, and skills needed?

- Who would this position report to?

- Who would be reporting to this position?

- Are there any items of priority that you would want me to focus on in this position?

- Are there any challenges, problems, or areas of concern facing this position?

- What were the strengths of the previous person in the position?

- How long has this position been available?

- What other departments does this position have shared responsibilities with?

- When do you expect to have the position filled?

This is only a *sample list* of questions. Develop your own list of questions that will not only help you in knowing what the company is seeking but will give you insight as to their HOT BUTTONS for a successful candidate. Use the answers to your advantage when talking about your background and how you can fulfill the company's need in this position.

If you are going to achieve excellence in big things, you develop the habit in little matters. Excellence is not an exception, it is a prevailing attitude.

—Colin Powell

Sample 3-E
Questions Interviewers Ask

Below are some typical and some not-so-typical questions to know about yourself. You should be prepared to answer without a long pause or hesitant posture.

Personal

- Tell me about yourself.

- What are your hobbies?

- Why did you choose to interview with our company?

- Describe your ideal job.

- What do you have to offer us?

- What do you consider your greatest strengths?

- What do you consider your weaknesses?

- What is your definition of success? Failure?

- Have you ever had any failures? What did you learn from them?

- Which accomplishment are you most proud of? Why?

- Who is your role model? Why?

- How does your college education or work experience relate to this job?

- What motivates you most in a job?

- Have you had difficulty getting along with a former supervisor/coworker and how did you handle it?

- Have you ever spoken before a group of people? How large?

- Why should we hire you rather than another candidate?

- What do you know about our company (products or services)?

- Where do you want to be in five years? Ten years?

- Do you plan to return to school for further education?

- What do you do to relieve stress?

- What motivates you?

Education

- Why did you choose this major?

- Why did you choose to attend your college or university?

- Do you think you received a good education? In what ways?

- In which campus activities did you participate?

- Which classes in your major did you like best? Least? Why?

- Which elective classes did you like best? Least? Why?

- What do you do to stay current in your field?

- If you were to start over, what would you change about your education?

- Do your grades accurately reflect your ability? Why or why not?

- Were you financially responsible for any portion of your college education?

Experience

- What job-related skills have you developed?

- Did you work while going to school? In what positions?

- What did you learn from those work experiences?

- What did you enjoy most about your last position? Least?

- Have you ever quit a job? Why?

- Give an example of a situation where you provided a solution for an employer.

- Give an example of a time when you worked under deadline pressure.

- Have you ever done any volunteer work? What kind?

- How do you think a former supervisor would describe you?

- How do you think a subordinate would describe you?

Career Related

- Do you prefer to work under supervision or on your own?

- What management style suits your personality?

- Would you be successful working with a team?

- Do you prefer large or small organizations? Why?

- What other types of positions are you considering?

- How do you feel about working in a structured environment?

- Are you able to multitask?

- How do you feel about working overtime?

- How do you feel about travel?

- How do you feel about the possibility of relocating?

- Are you willing to work flex-time?

- How would you describe your work habits?

Behavioral

- What goals have you set for yourself, and how are you planning to achieve them?

- Who or what has had the greatest influence in your career?

- Describe a situation in which you had to persuade someone to see things your way.

- What were the biggest challenges/problems you encountered in college? How did you handle them?

- Tell me about a class in which you were part of a study group. What role did you play in the group meetings?

- What was the toughest academic decision you have had to make? How did you make that decision?

- What kind of work experience has been the most valuable to you and why?

- Describe a time when a team member came to you for help. What was the situation? How did you respond?

- Tell me about a time when you had to deal with someone whose personality was different from yours.

- Have you ever been in a situation where someone regarded you as a threat? Describe the situation and tell how you handled it.

- Give me an example of when you had to be relatively quick in coming to a decision.

- Give me an example where you had to carry out a directive you did not agree with.

- How are you conducting your job search and how will you go about making your decision?

- What kind of situations put you under pressure, and how do you handle them?

- Tell me about a work accomplishment you are especially proud.

- What is the most important lesson you have learned in or out of school?

- Describe a time when you had to go beyond the call of duty to get the job done.

- Describe a time when you saw a problem and took the initiative to correct it rather than waiting for someone else to do it.

- Give examples to convince me that you can adapt to a wide variety of situations, people, and environments.

- What makes you the best person for this job?

- Tell me about a leadership role you had in an extracurricular activity. How did you lead?

- Tell me about your most successful presentation and what made it stand out.

- Describe a time when it was especially important to make a good impression on a customer. How did you go about doing it?

- Tell me about a meeting where you provided technical expertise. How did you ensure that everyone understood?

- Describe a time when you took a risk that you later regretted.

- How do you communicate with your supervisors? Peers? Subordinates?

- What do you say or do when someone reporting to you has made a significant (serious, costly) mistake?

Blueprint #3-3
The Interview

MATERIALS NEEDED

Pad (paper) and pen

Questions to Ask (*Sample 3-D*)

Résumé

Handkerchief or tissues

Proper attire and grooming

Positive attitude

PREP TIME

One (1) to two (2) hours

DIRECTIONS

- Dress appropriately (lay out your clothes the night before). Do not use perfumes, colognes, or scented aftershave, as some people have allergic reactions.

- Arrive at least five minutes early for your interview. It is not fashionable to be late!

- Relax. In fact, the goal of the intense preparation for the interview is exactly that: to be relaxed before you go in. But the most important thing is to be confident. The confident person is the relaxed person—and confidence sells! Preparation and practice are the keys to self-confidence.

- Display a positive attitude to everyone you meet, including the receptionist.

- Use a handkerchief or tissue if you need to sneeze. Do not sneeze into your hand. The interviewer might not want to shake hands with you later!

- If asked, give a copy of your résumé to the interviewer. If not asked, leave a copy AFTER THE INTERVIEW has concluded.

- Have prewritten questions with you during the interview (*Sample 3-D*).

- Always keep pen and paper handy. Write down important information, questions you might have during the interview, or cross off questions you have previously written down if they have been answered (*Sample 3-D*).

- Do not interrupt the interviewer while he/she is speaking; be a good listener. Let the interviewer ask you whatever questions he/she deems necessary.

- Control the interview—but be subtle. Keep the flow of the interview moving forward without going stale.

- Be brief, direct, concise, and to the point with your answers.

- Stick to the business of why you are there. No flowery pleasantries. Do not give long stories or more information than asked.

- Do not discuss compensation on the first interview. If it does come up, use the Negotiation Script during Interview (*Sample 4-B*).

- If the interviewer says, "Tell me about your background," respond with no more than a two- to three-minute, very simple overview. DO NOT go into detail, as you do not know what the interviewer wants.

- When it's your turn to speak, do your own "discovery interview," asking questions about the position and the company. Use the sample Questions to Ask (*Sample 3-D*) and any others you have written down during the interview.

- Once you are informed about the position and the company's needs, *you can go into detail* about your specific experiences, successes, and the accomplishments you have had that directly address those issues the employer is most concerned about.

- At the conclusion of the interview, ask, "Is there anything in my background that you might have some concerns or questions about, or anything that could preclude us from continuing our conversation?"

- The time to overcome any concerns or objections is when you are face-to-face. After you leave, the interviewer might come to a wrong conclusion about an issue in your background and you would not have had the opportunity to respond accordingly.

Interview Observations

Inexperienced interviewers do not always know what questions to ask.

Interviewers are often less prepared than the interviewee.

Hiring decisions are sometimes made based on impressions rather than facts.

SUMMARY

This step is like designing a new building! Successful contractors make preparations in advance. They know and use the right architects, engineers, electricians, and other trades, in the proper sequence, to get the expected results. Do your homework to learn about the company that you will be interviewing with, as it could make the difference between losing or winning the job. If you are properly prepared, the interview will go well.

CONCLUSION

Follow the blueprints in this chapter, and you will do exceedingly well. It is essentially just like building a house: follow the directions and you will get consistent results. But if you leave the foundation out, the results could be predictably disastrous.

NOTES

_____

_____

_____

_____

_____

_____

There is time for everything.

—Thomas A. Edison

Blueprint #3-4
The Follow-Up

MATERIALS NEEDED

Paper and pen

Word processor

Notes from interview

PREP TIME

Thirty (30) minutes to one (1) hour

DIRECTIONS

- Reflect on the interview and write down everything you felt uncomfortable with. This could be the company, the people you met, the questions you were asked, or even, your own answers or how you responded.

- Learn from this process. What do you need to do to improve? This improvement could be in scheduling interviews that do not fit for your background, the response you gave to certain questions asked, or how you handled yourself.

- Follow-up with a thank-you note. Amazingly, few candidates ever follow up after the interview is over (*Sample 3-F*). This is a great opportunity to get your name in front of the interviewer again! It also tells the interviewer that you have good communication skills, solid follow-through technique, and that you are serious about the job!

- If you didn't get the contact information during the interview or from the business card, simply call back and ask the receptionist, if one is available.

SUMMARY

You've had the interview and mailed your follow-up letter. What do you do now? For the most part, wait. Do not worry or fret about the job.

NOTES

_____

_____

_____

_____

_____

_____

_____

_____

Sample 3-F
Follow-Up Letter

Company Name

Name of Interviewer

Address

City, State, Zip

Date

Dear _____,

Thank you for the opportunity to interview with you for the position of _____. I am extremely interested in continuing our discussion. I will make myself available for any follow-up questions you might have. I can be reached by phone at home _____, cell _____, or by email _____. I look forward to another meeting with you.

Again, I appreciate the time you took with me.

Sincerely,

Your name

Your address

CHAPTER 4—NEGOTIATION

Successfully Reaching Agreement

Introduction

Several days or maybe a week or two have passed since you interviewed for a job. You might get a letter in the mail, or you might get a phone call. Congratulations! You have been offered the job. A sense of pride, accomplishment, and relief overcomes you. All your hard work and preparation has paid off. But remember, the job offer is only the beginning. Now the negotiations begin.

Negotiations for what, you might wonder. This is the final process in your new job search, but many potential employees are not even aware of this important step. This chapter will go into greater detail on this last and extremely important part of your job/career search.

What Is Negotiating?

According to the *Wall Street Journal,* "About 40% of job seekers may start work at lower pay than they should get because they're inept at salary negotiations." This is reason enough for all of us to investigate the art of negotiating. In this chapter, you will learn some secrets of negotiating for a better position, more money, and other very important benefits and perks.

The primary goal of negotiations is to reach an agreement, not necessarily just to win a position. When you think about it, we negotiate all the time. We negotiate with our children about assigned tasks, with our neighbors, with our coworkers, and we also negotiate when we are in the process of discussing compensation. The journey through successful negotiations is one of excitement, insight, and rewards.

Think for a moment about the jobs you have had. How did the job search go? How did the process of negotiating compensation go? There were probably many times during those negotiations when you wished you felt more comfortable and "safe." The truth is, we all feel that way during stressful situations, and negotiations can be stressful. In order to feel more comfortable in the future, it is important to understand some "in's and out's."

Some items to consider when negotiating your compensation package:

- Job Responsibilities

- Salaries

- Promotions

- Bonuses

- Vacations

- Projects

- Schedules

- Overtime

- Perks

- Benefits

- Title

- Location

The above items and probably many more in the workplace are good uses for negotiation. For example, if your boss needs a project completed by a scheduled date, and you know that date is not possible, it would be in your best interest to negotiate for a more reasonable date that you can meet. If you simply accept the requested date, you will not have the success you might have had if you had negotiated a more realistic date.

Negotiating is not to be confused with arguing. Remember that negotiating is "reaching a mutual agreement about an issue." What we desire in these transactions is a win-win solution. By approaching negotiations with a positive attitude, you will have a win-win, not a win-lose result. The key to achieving this goal is to strive for mutual gain, rather than believing that there must always be a winner and a loser.

Blueprint #4-1
Preparing for Negotiations

MATERIALS NEEDED

Paper and pen

Chair, desk, and light

Quiet place

Imagery for Negotiations (*Worksheet 4-A*)

Results from Knowing and Believing in Yourself (*Worksheet 4-B*)

PREP TIME

Four (4) to five (5) hours

DIRECTIONS

- Find a quiet place to begin Imagery for Negotiations (*Worksheet 4-A*).

- Think about what your work means to you. Is it truly a means of satisfaction to you, or is it simply a means to pay the bills and buy the things that are important to you? Determine what motivates you. Is this just a job, or is it a career? It is important to know this before you enter negotiations.

- Complete the worksheet about Knowing and Believing in Yourself (*Worksheet 4-B*). This supports what you will be negotiating for.

- Arrive at a compensation range for the position you have or will be interviewing for (*Worksheet 4-C*).

- From all the information you have gathered, develop a positive attitude and confidence that you know what the position is worth, but, more important, you will know what you are worth.

SUMMARY

Now all your work is about to pay off. Do not skip anything in this blueprint. To do so could result in a negotiation, long-term effect. For example, say your compensation range is approximately $50,000 per year.

Through solid negotiations you were able to get an additional 10 percent or $55,000. Now, suppose for the next two years you receive a pay increase of 5 percent. During the two years you will have earned $5,512.50 more than if you had accepted the $50,000. This blueprint is great. Follow the directions, and you will enjoy the results.

Worksheet 4-A
Imagery for Negotiations

Find a quite place where you feel comfortable. Sit comfortably and close your eyes; relax your body. Think of your upcoming salary/job negotiations meeting. Breathe deeply—feel yourself relaxing. Think of your prospective employer discussing the position and salary with you. You discuss the position and the desired salary—the salary you want and deserve. Think of it only in positive terms. You are receiving the salary offer you want, and the end result will be for your highest good. Continue to breathe deeply and focus on the negotiations and the positive outcome.

Worksheet 4-B
Knowing and Believing in Yourself

To be in the right frame of mind to negotiate, the first step is to sit down and review all your activities for the past year.

Identify Your Accomplishments

- What were your three most important/greatest accomplishments during the past year?

- What did you create?

- What process(es) did you improve?

- What did you put into effect?

- Who/What is better because of your actions?

- What did you reduce?

- What do your past performance appraisals reflect about you?

- Why would you be a valuable employee for any company?

- What would your last boss say about you?

- What do you "bring to the table" for your potential new company?

Put Your Requirements on Paper

Establishing Your Needs

Amy Black sat in the Human Resource manager's office. She had been offered the job, and they were getting to the salary part. This was always the part she disliked. She never felt comfortable discussing money. Besides, wasn't it already determined? She couldn't change anything, or could she?

Make a list of everything you want in preparation for discussion of compensation. As mentioned earlier, one of the rules or guidelines for preparation of compensation negotiation is to put it down on paper. Itemize the dollar estimate of everything in your previous compensation package. When asked how you came up with those figures, you can explain in detail from your worksheet.

Before you even go into an interview, know what you want and what concessions you are willing to make. Set your negotiating limits. Know the approximate salary level you want and feel you are worth, and settle on a reasonable, realistic salary. When working at lower- and middle-management levels, it is possible to ask and get from 10–20 percent more than what the interviewer is offering. In all cases, except when you are starting over in a new career, always aim for a higher salary than your previous job. It is important that your résumé show upward movement.

Prepare, prepare, and prepare! When the interviewer asks, "Why?" it is not only important to have good reasons, but also to have facts and figures for your request. If, for example, the interviewer says the company never pays more than the mentioned salary, you might be able to suggest reasons for you to be the exception. You have done your research; you have checked trade magazines, talked to people at the company and/or in the same industry. It is important that you get the facts prior to negotiating.

Do Your Homework

Know what you are talking about. Prior to the interview, you should have researched the company on the Internet and/or at the library. After the interview, you should know even more. By the time an offer comes, you should know comparable salaries at other companies, and, if possible, comparable salaries at this company. You should also know some of the education and experience others in your potential position possess. You'll know what is reasonable to ask and what constitutes a credible offer.

Maintaining a Positive Attitude

A positive attitude will carry you much further than a negative one. Although it's sometimes difficult, there are ways to develop and keep a positive attitude. Make enthusiasm a daily habit. Replace those negative thoughts in your head with positive affirmations.

Don't let negative people determine your self-worth. Earlier, we discussed the value of knowing yourself. Strong self-esteem comes from knowing who you are.

Worksheet 4-C
Establishing Your Needs

It's best to list the individual items so you don't leave anything out during the negotiation process. Earlier you completed exercises (*Worksheet 4-B*) that revealed information about yourself. This is another exercise to be done prior to negotiations

Lowest acceptable base salary _____

Relocation expenses _____

Position title _____

Starting date_____

Benefits

Allowance _____

Insurance _____

Cell Phone _____

Computer/Internet_____

Expense Account _____

Bonus Program _____

Perks

Club Membership _____

Stock Options/Grants _____

Equity _____

Severance Package _____

Retirement Plan/401k _____

Blueprint #4-2
The Negotiation Process

MATERIALS NEEDED

Paper and pen

Positive attitude

Smile

Self-confidence

Helpful Tips during Negotiations (*Sample 4-A*)

Establishing Your Needs (*Worksheet 4-C*)

Questions You Might Be Asked (*Worksheet 4-D*)

PREP TIME

As long as it takes with the hiring company

DIRECTIONS

- Establish strong people skills in the areas of eye contact, pleasant voice, listening, and empathy (*Sample 4-A*)**.**

- Don't attempt to negotiate on your first interview.

- After the initial interview and/or offer, be certain you want to work for the company and would welcome an offer. Go through the decision-making process (Chapter 1). List the pros and cons and follow the five steps for making decisions.

- Always, always (if you can), let the other person go first in the negotiation process.

- When made an offer, don't accept on the spot; take time to pray and think it over.

- Always get the offer in writing prior to any negotiations or acceptance. Once in writing you'll know the company is serious about hiring you.

- Look over the written offer in detail. Make a list of items that you wish to negotiate. These items could also include benefits and perks that have not been included.

- Remember, these negotiating skills are the same skills the company will be hiring you for; so don't disappoint them with your ability now (*Worksheet 4-D* and *Sample 4-B*).

- Know when to back off and not push beyond what the position is worth. You should have a very good idea if you completed Blueprint #4-1 on Preparing for Negotiations. If you do push too far, you risk losing the offer.

- Companies will usually offer a compensation that is lower than their established range for the position; they know that most people will try to negotiate for more. Don't disappoint them. Ask and you might receive!

- Start the negotiation with the largest or most significant item first: usually this will be the base salary. Don't spend time negotiating for the use of a cell phone when you know the base salary is too low.

- Give a range higher than where you want to be; usually you don't get everything you ask for.

- Be self-confident when you negotiate. If not, it'll show.

- Don't stat,: "If you pay me more, I'll accept." This is giving the company an ultimatum! You will lose.

- Give the company options, not a "do this or else" statement.

- Once all items have been mutually agreed to, request a new offer letter confirming this agreement.

- If all items in the new offer letter are correct, call to accept the position. Sign the offer letter and send a copy back confirming your verbal acceptance.

SUMMARY

Everything you have done, prepared for, and practiced will now pay off. Don't leave out any materials needed.

If sand is left out of concrete, guess what happens! If flour is left out of the cake mix, guess what happens! Don't skip any steps in the blueprints, as the results could be—well, at this point, you can probably guess.

Negotiating is an art. It is a technique that most people are embarrassed to use. Learn it and use it, as it will pay off. You will gain a greater respect from the people you negotiate with if you are honest and fair.

Worksheet 4-D
Questions You Might Be Asked

You don't have to give complete answers in this exercise; however, you do need to give some thought to these questions. Take a few moments and jot down some information for each question. Your responses should be organized and informative, and should answer the question thoroughly.

- Why do you want to work for this company?

- What are your salary requirements?

- When will you be able to start?

- Where do you want to be in five years?

- Why should we hire you?

Sample 4-A
Helpful Tips during Negotiations

DON'T use words such as

- I can't
- I think I can
- If only
- I have to
- Hate
- Difficult
- I'll try
- Should have
- Problem
- I, Me, My

DO use words such as

- I will
- Next time
- Opportunity
- You, your
- Challenging
- I want to
- I can
- Motivated
- Will do
- Excited

Project a Positive Attitude By—

- Smiling

- Using a firm handshake

- Watching your body language

- Sitting tall

- Speaking clearly

- Asking questions

Ask Questions

Keep the interviewer engaged in conversation by asking questions. There are positive ways to ask questions. Let's examine a few.

- Edit your questions for any tone (vocal inflection, sarcasm intonations) that could be demeaning or cause defensiveness.

- Listen intently. Use your "inner ear" to hear emotion and intent.

- Use the magic of *why* and *what* questions to find out why people believe what they believe. Please note here, do not just ask *"Why?"* as you will put the person on the defensive to justify his/her answer. Instead, say something like, "Just so I can understand, what would be the reason for not considering _____?"

- Use pronouns reflecting mutual gain (we, us, ours), and involve the other person in mutual problem solving with your questions.

You are responsible for creating your own positive image. Take responsibility for sending the message that shows others you are a qualified, intelligent, self-confident, and caring person, who will be an excellent team player.

NOTES

_____

_____

_____

_____

Sample 4-B
Negotiation Script during Interview

Employer: How much are you looking to earn in this position?

You: I'm currently earning (give what you actually are, or have been, earning). Don't offer any other additional information.

Employer: I would like to know what your expectations are for your compensation if we go forward. How much do you want to earn in this job?

You: (Again, respond with what you are currently earning or have been earning, then add) What I'm seeking is a job opportunity first and not just the compensation. I'm sure if we both want to go forward, we'll be able to come up with something that works for both of us.

Offer Extended

You: I'm really excited about your company and the opportunity offered to me. I had the time to review the offer and have a few items I would like to discuss with you.

Employer: What are the items you have some concern about?

You: The starting base appears a bit too low as I am seeking a base salary in the $_____ range. I would also need assistance with relocation expenses and an auto allowance.

Employer: I'll revisit these items and send you a revised offer letter.

You: Thank you, I look forward to receiving the letter.

Should You Accept a Salary Cut?

The question of accepting a lower base salary in a new position confronts more and more people changing jobs, especially in today's market.

Accepting a lower salary might be inevitable if you are a victim of a layoff or you can't leave the area. Remember, the salary scale for larger companies are often higher than those for smaller companies.

The decision to accept a lower salary often makes sense, particularly if you are changing careers. In most cases, compensation relates to the amount of experience you have in a particular field. You could negotiate for other non-cash items (perks, benefits), which are forms of compensation. This could be a valid reason to accept a lower starting salary.

Far and away the best prize that life offers is the
chance to work hard at work worth doing.

—Theodore Roosevelt

Blueprint #4-3
After the Negotiation

MATERIALS NEEDED

Paper and pen

Quite place

Negotiations Assessment (*Worksheet 4-E*)

Negotiation Script during Interview (*Sample 4-B*)

Resignation Letter (*Sample 4-C*)

PREP TIME

One (1) to two (2) hours

DIRECTIONS

- Sitting alone in a quiet place, reflect on the entire negotiation process.

- Read over and answer the questions on Negotiations Assessment (*Worksheet 4-E*). Be honest, as this will help you with any future negotiations.

- Be certain that you have signed and returned the offer letter. If not accepting, send a rejection letter.

- If you accepted, draft a letter of resignation (if needed) to provide to your current employer (*Sample 4-C*).

Summary

The importance of understanding the art of negotiations cannot be minimized. Whether you are seeking your first job, a new career, better salary, perks and benefits, or better employee reviews, knowing how to negotiate to get them is of the utmost importance. Now that you know how the art of negotiations is played, the process of getting a job should be much less stressful. You have learned skills that will be invaluable to you in the employment world.

HOMEWORK

I hope that your negotiation process will be productive. No matter the result, it is still a wonderful learning experience. Take a few moments to reflect on the negotiation process and answer the questions on the Worksheet 4-E.

NOTES

_____

_____

_____

_____

_____

_____

_____

_____

Sample 4-C
Resignation Letter

[Your Name]
[Street • City • State • Zip Code]
[Phone # • Fax phone # • Messages phone # • Email]

[Date today]

[Recipient's name]
[Company name]
[Address]
[Address]
[Address]

Dear [Recipient's name]:

Please accept this letter as my notice of resignation, effective [date].

This wasn't an easy decision, because I am grateful for the rewarding employment I've had with [Company name]. But after long hours of consideration, my decision is now final and I have accepted a position with another company.

Sincere thanks and best wishes for the future,

[Sign here]

[Your name, title]
cc [Names for copies]

Worksheet 4-E
Negotiations Assessment

Self-Assessment

Read the following list of negotiation statements and circle the ones you agree with. The ones you don't circle are the areas you will want to improve.

- I will be better able to negotiate the salary I desire in my next job.

- I have improved my negotiation skills.

- I believe I have the "right" people skills for negotiating.

- I know how to negotiate a salary when offered a new job.

- I understand how to negotiate for a better benefits package.

- I know how to control my stress during negotiations.

- I know when to negotiate, and I understand how negotiations work.

- I feel good about other negotiations I have handled.

- I understand the timing of negotiating items in a compensation package.

Areas That Need Improvement

Evaluate how you handled different negotiation situations (salary, budget, schedule).

Situation_____

- Did I "clam up" and let whatever happens happen?

- Did I take charge of the situation and start reaching for agreement, or did I fall somewhere in between?

- Did I get what I wanted?

- Did I get the salary I requested?

- Did I get the job, shift, work schedule, etc. I requested?

- How did I feel during the negotiation process?

ABOUT THE AUTHOR

In the early 1990s, Dennis founded Caruso & Associates, Inc. This firm provides executive recruiting and human resources services for numerous clients on a national and international level.

His career as an executive recruiter began in 1983 with a large retainer-based search firm where he developed his expertise in several industries including real estate and finance. Before that, Dennis was chief operating officer and chief financial officer for a multifaceted, 50-year-old, construction materials manufacturer, a publicly traded company. Prior to that position, he served as vice president, finance and administration for an entrepreneurial enterprise that manufactured, marketed, and distributed energy control devices. His career began as a certified public accountant for PricewaterhouseCoopers, LLP, formerly, Coopers & Lybrand.

Dennis graduated magna cum laude from the University of Florida majoring in accounting and business administration. He has also served as chairman of a review panel for faith-based initiative programs in Washington, DC.